Cooks Academy Cookbook

Recipes from the Cookery School

Cooks Academy Cookbook

Recipes from the Cookery School

VANESSA GREENWOOD

GILL & MACMILLAN

Gill & Macmillan Ltd
Hume Avenue
Park West
Dublin 12
with associated companies throughout the world
www.gillmacmillan.ie

978 07171 4395 5

Photographs by Hugh McElveen, except pages ii, xii, xv, 18-19, 75, 158, 167-8
Food styled by Sharon Hearne-Smith
Props supplied by Arnotts, Habitat, Marks & Spencer, Murphy Sheehy Fabrics
Index compiled by Cover to Cover
Book design and typesetting by Graham Thew
Printed by GraphyCems Ltd, Spain

The paper used in this book comes from the wood pulp of managed forests. For
every tree felled, at least one tree is planted, thereby renewing natural resources.

A CIP catalogue record for this book is available from the British Library.

5 4 3 2 1

Dedication

To my Grandma, Sarah Platt.

Table of Contents

Foreword

SINCE COOKS ACADEMY OPENED its doors in 2005, our customers have embraced the food ethos we have endeavoured to create.

With so much time and money spent on eating out, we wanted to bring families back into the kitchen together to enjoy food, conversation and each others' company. When you come from a foodie family, you might take the good food you grew up with or the effortlessness of cooking dinner for granted. In our case, food was always central to our lives and our relationships and it is our passion.

When I travel, I want to check out the local fish or vegetable market, the honest pub grub, the nearest cookery school and even go out fishing or collecting mussels and befriending the local fishermen for the odd lobster or some crabs.

Classes in the school are packed with wonderful people who we have come to know and befriend. Every day, we are inspired by their enthusiasm and feedback about our school, our tutors and their feeling that they are among friends. Our ambition is to instil a passion for home cooking and we love to hear stories of our students' kitchen escapades after we have sent them off armed with great recipes and a zeal for cooking for their family and friends.

In this cookbook we want to share some of the popular recipes (including many of our old favourites) enjoyed by our students in the cookery school. Using accessible ingredients and a down-to-earth cooking approach, we want everyone to enjoy making the recipes, gain confidence in their cooking ability, build their repertoire and, most of all, learn something new.

For us at Cooks Academy, cooking is simply about unleashing your creative talents and living a healthier lifestyle by avoiding processed foods.

About Cooks Academy

COOKS ACADEMY was founded in 2005 by Vanessa and Tim Greenwood, who decided to set up a purpose-built, professionally run cookery school in Dublin. The school mainly caters to the amateur cookery enthusiast. Typical classes start with basic and essential cookery and move on through breads, pastries, seafood to entertaining and onward to ethnic cuisines. Classes are held in the evenings, during the week, on Saturdays and Sundays. As with this book, the emphasis throughout is on the type of food people might like to cook at home.

The school runs a month-long Professional Certificate Course. Designed to upskill swiftly and systematically, it is a favourite with aspiring food entrepreneurs, lifelong cooks, young cooks and the hospitality trade.

So drop into Cooks Academy sometime or log on to the website (www.CooksAcademy.com). You'll be surprised at the diversity of culinary know-how on offer.

Acknowledgements

THANKS TO ALL the team at Cooks Academy who helped this book along the way.

Thanks to Sarah Liddy at Gill and Macmillan for her professionalism, Hugh McElveen for the wonderful photography and Sharon Hearne-Smith for her fabulous styling expertise. Thanks also to Karen Convery for her artistic flair and dedication.

Special thanks to our many wonderful tutors in the school, especially Rozanne Stevens, whose diverse salads and whole food cookery are truly exceptional; to Gráinne Wall, whose ability to add a contemporary twist to a dish is awesome and to Ivor O'Connor for adding a touch of class. Thanks to Colette Carty and Bert Wright for guiding us through the publishing world.

Also to all the home cooks whose amazing cooking has inspired recipes in the school. To Roberta, my stepmother, the most prolific recipe tester I have ever met; to my dad, who as soon as we could reach the stove taught us the life-long skill of making white sauce and gravy; to Siobhan Dillon, who always brought something nice in a biscuit tin on our holidays; to Anne Montgomery, whose shellfish platters are legendary; to Michael and Jenny Greenwood for the free access to the family farmers' market in their garden. To my late Aunty Joan, who always had a welcoming bowl of homemade soup heating on the Aga, and to Germana Lambertini, whose Italian cooking is a joy to behold.

But not least, thanks to Tim, my husband, for all the encouragement and who has loved creating Cooks Academy as much as I have.

Recipe Notes

Recipes included in this book take the following into account.

- Always read through a recipe from start to finish before cooking.
- Preparation of ingredients is stated in the ingredients list to assist cooks to become organised before they start cooking.
- All lettuce and herbs should be washed.
- Unless stated, chicken breasts are skinless and vegetables such as potatoes and carrots are peeled.
- All herbs are fresh unless stated as dried.
- Ginger is always peeled.
- Garlic cloves are always peeled unless otherwise stated.
- Feel free to substitute vegetable stock when cooking for vegetarians.
- When handling chillies or raw meats, it is often advisable to wear thin vinyl gloves and avoid rubbing your eyes.
- 1 tsp = 5ml
- 1 tbsp = 15ml
- When frying onions, add more oil as required.
- It's worth keeping one expensive bottle of extra virgin olive oil that you like in your store cupboard and using it when a good-quality extra virgin olive oil is used in a recipe (especially when making salad dressings).

Equipment

We have assumed that most kitchens are equipped with a rolling pin, pastry brush, slotted spoon, baking trays, fine graters, measuring spoons, heavy-based saucepans and a good set of sharp knives.

Kitchen Consumables

It is always handy to have the following in your kitchen: cling film, tin foil, parchment paper (or greaseproof paper) and thin vinyl gloves (for handling chillies).

CHAPTER I
Soups

Quick Gazpacho

Serves 4

A summer-inspired soup which is great served with some crusty bread. It can be made all year round with this method using tinned tomatoes. However, if you have really flavoursome fresh tomatoes, use them instead.

1 x 400g tin chopped tomatoes

1 tbsp sherry vinegar

2 cloves garlic, crushed

$1/2$ cucumber, roughly chopped

$1/2$ small red onion, chopped

400ml good-quality tomato juice

1 red pepper, deseeded, deribbed and roughly chopped

3 tbsp extra virgin olive oil

1 tbsp honey

10 drops Tabasco sauce

1 tsp Worcestershire sauce

tiny diced tomato, red onion and chopped mint leaves, to garnish (optional)

salt and freshly cracked black pepper

1 Put the chopped tomatoes, vinegar, garlic, cucumber, red onion, tomato juice and red pepper in a blender and whiz to a purée (for an even smoother consistency, pass through a sieve 2 to 3 times). With the motor still running, slowly add the olive oil through the feeder along with the honey, Tabasco and Worcestershire sauce. Season to taste. Cover and chill in the fridge for at least 2 hours.

2 Serve in small soup bowls or cups, garnishing with any combination of tiny diced vegetables, a slick of good-quality extra virgin olive oil and a good grinding of black pepper.

WHEN BUYING GARLIC, AVOID BULBS WITH GREEN SPROUTS – THEY'RE NOT FRESH.

Seafood Chowder

Serves 4

This dish is a real hit with students on our seafood workshops.

200g fish (e.g. 150g salmon, 50g smoked haddock)

50g butter

1 potato, diced small

1 carrot, diced small

1 stick celery, diced small

1 small leek, finely sliced

25g flour

1 litre fish stock (see p. 192)

75ml cream

100g cooked and peeled medium-sized prawns

5 sprigs flat leaf parsley, chopped

pinch paprika

salt and freshly cracked black pepper

1 Using a fish tweezers, pin bone and remove the skin from the fish before cutting the flesh into chunks. Refrigerate.

2 Melt the butter in a medium saucepan and on a low to medium heat, sweat the potato, carrot, celery and leek for 10 minutes, using a cartouche (paper lid pressed down on top of the vegetables). Season with salt and pepper and stir occasionally.

3 Stir in the flour and cook for 2 minutes.

4 Raise the heat, then gradually add the stock, stirring well to prevent lumps from forming. Bring to the boil.

5 Add the fish (except the prawns, as they will shrivel up if overcooked) and simmer for a further 5 minutes until the fish is cooked.

6 Stir in the cream and check seasoning once again. Just before serving, stir in the cooked prawns and the chopped parsley. Serve with a pinch of paprika on top.

....

A CARTOUCHE IS A PAPER LID PLACED ON TOP OF WHATEVER YOU'RE COOKING THAT SLOWS DOWN THE REDUCTION OF COOKING LIQUIDS IN A POT. TO MAKE ONE, WITH A PAIR OF SCISSORS CUT A SQUARE PIECE OF PARCHMENT A GOOD BIT BIGGER THAN THE POT. FOLD IT IN HALF DIAGONALLY, THEN AGAIN TWICE MORE AT RIGHT ANGLES TO THE LONGER SIDE OF THE TRIANGLE. HOLD THE POINT OF THE PAPER AS CLOSE TO THE CENTRE POINT OF THE POT AS POSSIBLE AND, CUTTING AROUND THE RIM, REMOVE THE EXCESS PAPER FROM THE CARTOUCHE. OPEN IT OUT AND YOU WILL HAVE A CIRCLE OF PAPER ROUGHLY THE SIZE OF YOUR POT. IF IT'S A LITTLE BIGGER THAN THE PAN, DON'T WORRY.

Butternut Squash Soup

Serves 4

People sometimes avoid squash because it can be a task to chop it safely. This method roasts the squash whole in the oven to bypass this problem and many of our students never look back. If you like a hint of warm spices, add 1 tsp of garam masala when frying the onion.

1 medium (800g) butternut squash

1 medium onion, chopped

40g butter

1 tsp fresh thyme leaves

1.1 litres hot chicken stock

freshly cracked sea salt and black pepper

SALTED ALMONDS

15g butter, melted

30g flaked almonds

sea salt

Preheat the oven to 180°C/350°F/gas mark 4.

1 Roast the squash whole in the oven for 30 minutes, without the skin browning. Remove from the oven and allow to cool fully before slicing into 4 lengths, deseeding, removing the skin and cutting the squash into large cubes.

2 Over a low heat, sweat the onion in butter for approximately 8 minutes, until softened.

3 Stir in the squash and thyme, followed by the hot stock. Season with salt and pepper. Bring to a low simmer for 10 minutes.

4 To prepare the salted almonds, roast the flaked almonds in the oven for 6 minutes until lightly toasted. Put the roasted almonds in a bowl, stir in the butter along with a sprinkling of sea salt and cool in the fridge for 2 minutes to harden.

5 Using a handheld blender, process the soup until smooth. Ladle into soup bowls and serve garnished with the salted almonds.

Golden Chicken Broth

Our Winter Soups and Casseroles course features a wonderful array of soups against which this soothing broth holds its own.

2 vine-ripened tomatoes

1.2 litres chicken stock, homemade is best (or use a low-salt brand)

10 saffron strands

1 carrot, peeled and diced small

1 x 200g chicken breast, sliced very thinly

10 sprigs flat leaf parsley, chopped

salt and freshly cracked black pepper

1 Remove the stalky eyes from the tomatoes, score a cross in each base, then immerse them in boiling water for 30 seconds before plunging them into cold water. Peel away the loosened skin, then quarter the flesh and deseed them. Dice up the tomato flesh and set aside.

2 If you are not using homemade stock, make up the stock in a saucepan, adding a small amount of boiling water first to form a paste, then add the remaining water and bring to the boil.

3 Add the saffron and carrot and simmer for a few minutes before adding the thinly sliced chicken and poaching it in the broth for 3 minutes, until cooked. Add the chopped parsley and check the seasoning.

4 Just before serving, place a spoonful of tomato in each bowl and ladle over the hot broth.

THOUGH GREAT FOR COLOUR, USE SAFFRON SPARINGLY, AS TOO MUCH CAN BE OVERPOWERING. DID YOU KNOW IT COMES FROM A FLOWER OF THE CROCUS FAMILY?

Spinach and Nutmeg Soup

Golden Chicken Broth

Spinach and Nutmeg Soup

Serves 4

It's worth buying the large leaf, stalky spinach from the farmers' market for this soup. We find it difficult to get it in supermarkets now.

25g butter

1 medium onion, chopped

1 clove garlic, crushed

1 litre chicken stock (or vegetable), hot

500g stalky spinach, washed, stalks left intact

nutmeg, freshly grated

cream, to serve

salt and freshly cracked black pepper

1 Melt the butter in a large saucepan and sweat the onion for 10 minutes over a medium heat. Add the crushed garlic towards the end.

2 Increase the heat and pour 100ml of hot stock into the saucepan before packing in the spinach.

3 Cover with a lid, removing it to stir occasionally. When the spinach has wilted, add the remaining stock. Bring to the boil and simmer over a low heat for 10 minutes.

4 Blend, season and add freshly grated nutmeg to taste.

5 Ladle into soup bowls and serve immediately with a generous swirl of cream.

YOU CAN CRUSH GARLIC WITH A DECENT-SIZED COOK'S KNIFE. CUT OFF THE ROOT END, THEN SQUASH THE BULB WITH THE SIDE OF THE KNIFE. PINCH THE SKIN OFF FROM THE OTHER END. AFTER YOU'VE PRACTISED THIS A FEW TIMES, THE SKIN SHOULD POP OFF IN ONE GO. THEN CHOP THE GARLIC FINELY, SPRINKLE WITH SOME TABLE SALT (TO GIVE THE KNIFE GRIP) AND PULP IT INTO A PASTE WITH THE SIDE OF YOUR KNIFE.

Mushroom Soup

Serves 4

I love a smooth, velvety mushroom soup and I find a food processor really achieves a great result.

30g butter

1 onion, finely sliced

750g very fresh mushrooms (or a mixture of varieties), wiped clean and roughly chopped

3 tbsp Madeira (or dry sherry)

1 tsp fresh thyme leaves (or tarragon)

800ml chicken stock (or vegetable), hot

250ml full-fat milk

cream and freshly chopped parsley, to serve

salt and freshly cracked black pepper

1 In a medium saucepan, melt the butter over a very low heat, add the onion and fry gently for 10 minutes, or until translucent. Increase the heat, add the mushrooms, Madeira and thyme and season well with salt and pepper. Cook for 3 minutes, or until the juices start to run. Add the hot stock and simmer for 10 minutes, stirring occasionally. Whiz the soup to a fine consistency.

2 Stir in the milk and check the seasoning. Simmer for another minute. Ladle into soup bowls and serve with a drizzle of cream and freshly chopped herbs.

IF YOU COOK WITH MUSHROOMS A LOT, INVEST IN A NYLON BRUSH TO CLEAN THEM WITH. IT'S BEST NOT TO WASH MUSHROOMS, AS FLAVOUR GETS LOST. IF YOU HAVE TO, WIPE THEM WITH A DAMP CLOTH.

Cherry Tomato, Carrot and Lentil Soup

Serves 4

This is a lovely soup and if you grow oregano in your herb patch, it will substitute wonderfully for the chopped parsley.

25g butter

1 tbsp olive oil

1 onion, diced

1 medium potato, peeled and diced

2 carrots, diced

500g cherry tomatoes, halved

60g red lentils (soaked for 4 hours, if possible)

1.2 litres chicken stock, hot

2 sprigs parsley, leaves chopped

cream, to serve

salt and freshly cracked black pepper

1 In a medium saucepan, heat the butter and olive oil. Sweat the onion over a gentle heat for 5 minutes, until translucent. Increase the heat and add the diced potato, carrots and tomatoes. Season well and stir over a medium heat for 5 minutes, until the tomato juices start to run and coat the other vegetables.

2 Add the lentils and stock, cover and bring to the boil, then simmer for 15 minutes. Liquidise to a smooth consistency with a handheld blender.

3 Ladle into soup bowls and serve garnished with cream and freshly chopped parsley.

SOAKING RED LENTILS MAKES THEM MORE DIGESTIBLE AND LESSENS THEIR COOKING TIME.

Celeriac, Apple and Cashel Blue Soup

Serves 4

If you can't get celeriac, try using celery instead, in which case I like to remove the stringy outer layer from each celery stalk using a wide vegetable peeler.

50g butter

1 medium leek (220g cut weight), white stalk only, washed and thinly sliced

350g celeriac, peeled and roughly chopped

2 apples, peeled, cored and diced

150g potato, peeled and diced

900ml vegetable stock, hot

100g Cashel Blue cheese, crumbled

1 tbsp chopped chives

75ml cream, whipped

salt and freshly cracked black pepper

1 Melt the butter in a medium heavy-based saucepan, add the leek and celeriac, cover with a cartouche (paper lid pressed down over the vegetables; see p. 4) and sweat for 10 minutes, until softened. Add the diced apple and cook for a further 3–4 minutes, stirring occasionally, and season well. Add the potato and hot stock, cover and bring to the boil, then reduce the heat to a simmer for a further 10 minutes or until the potato is cooked.

2 Whiz the soup with a handheld blender until smooth. Stir in the crumbled blue cheese and whiz once more.

3 Ladle into soup bowls and garnish with chopped chives and a generous dollop of whipped cream.

INSTEAD OF CHOPPING CHIVES, SNIP OFF THE REQUIRED LENGTHS WITH YOUR KITCHEN SCISSORS.

Tom Khaa Kai

Serves 4

This classic Thai soup is not meant to be overwhelmingly hot, but to have a sweet, salty, sour taste.

2 lemongrass stalks, white part only

5cm piece of galangal (or ginger)

2 chicken breasts (350g in total)

700–800ml reduced-fat coconut milk, shake the can to mix well

5 makrut lime leaves, roughly torn

2 shallots, finely sliced

100g button mushrooms, halved

2 tbsp fish sauce

1 tbsp brown sugar (or palm sugar)

10 cherry tomatoes, halved (leave whole if very small)

3 tbsp lime juice

2 red chillies, deseeded and finely sliced

20g coriander, leaves only

1 Remove the tough outer leaves from the lemongrass. Using the tip of a knife, cut along the length of the remaining inner part to form a tassel and bruise once with a rolling pin.

2 Peel the galangal (or ginger) and cut into thin round slices.

3 To prepare the chicken, lay the breasts between 2 layers of cling film and bash with a rolling pin, then remove the cling film and, on a chopping board, slice into pencil-thin strips.

4 Put the lemongrass, galangal (or ginger), coconut milk, lime leaves and shallots in a saucepan over a medium heat and bring to the boil.

5 Add the chicken, mushrooms, fish sauce and sugar and reduce the heat to a simmer, stirring constantly for 5 minutes, or until the chicken is cooked through.

6 Add the tomatoes, lime juice and most of the chillies (finely chopping the remaining slices to use later as a garnish) and simmer for 3 minutes only. Taste and adjust the seasoning.

7 Just before serving, remove any large pieces of lemongrass and lime leaves.

8 Stir through half the coriander leaves.

9 To serve, add coriander leaves and chopped chilli to each bowl and ladle over the hot soup.

GALANGAL HAS A DISTINCT PINE-LIKE, CITRUS FLAVOUR. WHILE GINGER DIFFERS IN TASTE, COOKS OFTEN USE IT AS A SUBSTITUTE FOR GALANGAL.

CHAPTER 2
Starters & Light Bites

Fried Calamari with a Crème Fraîche Dip

Serves 4

I can never resist this starter when I see it on a menu. For a twist, why not add chilli or garlic to the seasoned flour?

400g (approximately 3–4 tubes) medium squid tubes

100g plain flour

2 eggs, lightly whisked

3–4 tbsp sunflower oil (or to fill a pan to a depth of 5mm)

1 lemon, cut into wedges, to serve

salt and freshly cracked black pepper

CRÈME FRAÎCHE DIP

3 tbsp crème fraîche

2 tbsp sweet chilli sauce

1 Make the dip by mixing together the crème fraîche and sweet chilli sauce. Refrigerate.

2 Wash the squid tubes thoroughly and pat them dry with kitchen paper. Slice the tubes into 5cm rings. In a bowl, season the flour with salt and pepper. Mix the eggs into the flour, then dip the squid rings into the batter and coat thoroughly.

3 Not leaving the stove, pour the oil into a heavy-based frying pan to a depth of 5mm and heat until quite hot. Test a small ring first, and fry (but do not brown) the squid rings in 2 batches, placing the cooked squid on kitchen paper between batches (be careful not to overcook the squid). Just before serving, return all the squid to the pan to warm through. Serve immediately with the crème fraîche dip and a wedge of lemon.

WHEN YOU BUY SQUID, IT NORMALLY COMES AS JUST THE TUBES. IF YOU CAN GET THE TENTACLES, COOK THEM AS PER THE RECIPE. FOR MANY, THEY ARE THE MOST PRIZED PART. MANY ASIAN STORES STOCK SQUID WITH TENTACLES IN THEIR FROZEN SECTION.

Eggs Benedict

Serves 4

This classic brunch dish is also super with crumpets.

1 x quantity hollandaise sauce
(see p. 196)

2 tsp salt

4 large organic eggs

4 unsweetened English muffins,
sliced in half

8 thin slices smoked ham

1 tbsp finely chopped chives, to
garnish

1 Make up the hollandaise sauce and keep warm (see p. 196).
2 Add the salt to a small saucepan of simmering water. Stir to make a whirlpool, break in 1 egg and cook gently for 3 minutes. Lift out with a slotted spoon onto a plate and repeat with the other eggs.
3 Keep the water hot while you toast the muffin halves under the grill. Keep warm.
4 Just before serving, slide the eggs back into the hot water for 30 seconds to heat through, then lift out and drain on kitchen paper.
5 Divide the muffins between plates and top one muffin half with 1–2 slices of ham and an egg. Spoon over the warm hollandaise, garnish with chives and serve with the remaining muffin half.

SUBSTITUTE THE HAM WITH COOKED SPINACH FOR EGGS FLORENTINE OR SMOKED SALMON FOR EGGS ROYALE, AKA SALMON BENEDICT.

Chicken Satay Skewers

Makes 15 skewers

Ideal to serve as finger food at a party. Satay sauce is very versatile, so try beef or tofu instead of the chicken.

3 chicken breasts, cut into bite-sized pieces

1 tbsp soy sauce

2 tbsp groundnut oil (or peanut oil)

40g ginger, peeled and grated

2 cloves garlic, crushed

5 tbsp smooth peanut butter

1 tbsp caster sugar

2 tbsp soy sauce

2 tbsp Worcestershire sauce

2 tbsp toasted sesame oil

75ml chicken stock (or vegetable), hot

dash of Tabasco sauce, to taste

1 Place the chicken in a bowl and marinate with the soy sauce, groundnut oil and half of both the ginger and garlic. Refrigerate for 1 hour.

2 Meanwhile, soak some bamboo skewers in cold water for 1 hour.

3 In a small bowl, mix together the remaining ginger and garlic with the peanut butter, sugar, soy sauce, Worcestershire sauce and toasted sesame oil. Whiz to a paste in a food processor before adding the hot stock and continue until the mixture reaches a smooth consistency. Add Tabasco sauce to taste. Set aside half the sauce in a small bowl to use as a dip.

4 Remove the chicken from the fridge and pierce each piece with a skewer. Season with pepper. Under a medium grill, cook the chicken skewers for 8 minutes, turning to ensure they are cooked through. Brush the chicken with the remaining satay sauce and keep warm under a low grill. To serve, place the dip in the centre of a plate surrounded by chicken skewers.

Baba Ghanoush

Makes 200ml

This smooth aubergine purée is delightful when served with a mezze platter of dips, marinated olives, tabbouleh, falafel, cubes of cheese and warm pitta breads.

1 large aubergine

1 bulb garlic

2 tbsp lemon juice

1 tbsp tahini paste

1–2 tbsp good-quality extra virgin olive oil, as required

pinch paprika, to garnish

salt and freshly cracked black pepper

Preheat the oven to 200°C/400°F/gas mark 6.

1 Pierce the skin near the stem of the aubergine with a fork (so the aubergine does not burst during cooking) and roast the aubergine whole for 40 minutes, turning the aubergine once during cooking so the skin chars evenly.

2 Meanwhile, cut the bulb of garlic in half across the equator, drizzle olive oil over the cut surface and wrap in tinfoil. Roast in the oven for 25 minutes. Once it is cooked, squeeze the soft garlic flesh from one half (store the other half for use in gravies). Remove the aubergine from the oven when it is cooked, cut in half lengthways and scoop out the flesh with a spoon, discarding the skin.

3 In a small food processor (or use a handheld blender), blend the aubergine, garlic, lemon juice and tahini paste. Season generously with salt and pepper. Slowly mix in the oil, adding more as required until it forms a smooth, silky consistency.

4 Place in a small bowl and refrigerate for 3 hours before serving. To serve, garnish with a pinch of paprika and present as part of a mezze platter, or simply spread on warm crusty bread.

TAHINI PASTE IS A SAVOURY SPREAD MADE FROM FINELY GROUND SESAME SEEDS. IT IS USED MAINLY IN ORIENTAL, MIDDLE EASTERN AND AFRICAN CUISINES.

Quick Tuna Pâté

Makes 400g

Whip this pâté up in 2 minutes flat and serve as a pre-dinner dip with crudités, oatcakes, mini toasts or on top of thick slices of cucumber.

1 x 185g tin tuna, drained
225g cream cheese
1 tbsp lemon juice
freshly cracked black pepper
pinch paprika, to garnish
1 sprig of flat leaf parsley,
 to garnish

1 Blend the tuna and cream cheese until smooth (use either a food processor or place in a bowl and blend using a handheld blender).
2 Add lemon juice and season with pepper, to taste.
3 Transfer to a serving bowl and chill in the fridge until ready to serve.
4 To serve, garnish with a pinch of paprika and a sprig of parsley.

Garlic Mushrooms

Serves 4

Garlicky and delicious served either as a starter or with steak.

300g mushrooms, wiped clean
15g butter
1 tbsp olive oil
3 garlic cloves, chopped
2 tbsp white wine (or Madeira)
50ml cream
3 tbsp chopped curly parsley
 and/or thyme leaves
fresh crusty bread, warm, to
 serve
salt and freshly cracked black
 pepper

1 Remove the stalks from the mushrooms. Cut each mushroom in half, then each half into 3–4 wedges.
2 Over a medium-high heat, melt the butter in a wide heavy-based frying pan. When it begins to foam, add the mushrooms and sauté over a high heat (if the mushrooms start to liquefy, drain off and reserve this liquid).
3 Add the olive oil to the pan and then add the garlic. Season well with salt and pepper and stir for another minute.
4 Add the wine (and any reserved mushroom liquid) and simmer for 2 minutes, until the liquid has reduced.
5 Just before serving, stir in the cream over a high heat. Toss in the chopped parsley and/or thyme and serve with crusty bread.

AVOID BOILING THE MUSHROOMS IN THEIR OWN JUICES
BY USING A WIDE FRYING PAN

Fragrant Crab Cakes with Chilli Sauce

Serves 4

My girlfriends always go for crab cakes when they see them on a restaurant menu, so I know I can't go wrong serving these to my friends at home.

200g fresh cooked crabmeat

3 spring onions, finely sliced

10g fresh coriander, leaves coarsely chopped (reserve some sprigs for a garnish)

50g breadcrumbs

1 egg

1 red chilli, deseeded and finely chopped

1 red pepper, deseeded and quartered

25g sugar

1 tsp white wine vinegar

150ml water

1 tbsp sunflower oil

salt and freshly cracked black pepper

Preheat the oven to 180°C/350°F/gas mark 4.

1 Carefully pick through the crabmeat to remove any stray shell and break up any large lumps of crab. Squeeze out any excess liquid (the resulting consistency should be sticky).

2 In a large bowl, mix together the crabmeat, spring onions, coriander, breadcrumbs, egg and half the chilli. Season and mould the mixture into 3 round cakes per person.

3 Heat the grill to hot. Place the peppers on a baking sheet, skin side up, and grill until blackened and blistered (this might take anything from 5 to 15 minutes). Place in a bowl and cover immediately with cling film and leave for 20 minutes to cool (the cling film will trap the steam and loosen the skins). Once the skins have loosened, peel the peppers and discard the skin.

4 Heat the sugar, vinegar, water, red pepper and remaining chilli in a non-reactive saucepan and simmer for 10 minutes, until the liquid has thickened. Blend to a smooth purée using a handheld blender. Allow to cool.

5 Heat the sunflower oil in a pan and gently fry the cakes on both sides until golden, then cook in a hot oven for 8 minutes at 180°C/350°F/gas mark 4. Serve garnished with fresh coriander leaves and the chilli sauce.

TIMINGS FOR COOKING CRAB IN SIMMERING WATER:
CRABS UP TO 550G, 15 MINUTES;
CRABS UP TO 900G, 20 MINUTES;
CRABS UP TO 1.5KG, 25 MINUTES.
ANY LARGER CRAB: 30 MINUTES.

FOR BEST-QUALITY CRABMEAT, BEFRIEND A FISHERMAN
AT THE QUAYSIDE AND FIND OUT WHERE TO BUY CRABS
DIRECT FROM THEM. IT CAN BE TIME CONSUMING TO
EXTRACT THE CRABMEAT, BUT IF ON HOLIDAYS OR WITH A
BUNCH OF PEOPLE, IT'S A NICE THING TO DO OVER A GLASS
OF CRISP CHABLIS WHILE EXCHANGING A FEW YARNS.

Howth Sandwich

Serves 2

Tim's dad often reminisces about his fishing days in Howth. The fishermen used to rustle up these decadent sandwiches as a snack – what bounty!

12 Dublin Bay prawns

2 thick slices cut from a fresh white loaf (a soft Vienna roll is great)

15g butter

2 large free-range eggs

2 handfuls fresh rocket

drizzle of extra virgin olive oil

salt and freshly cracked black pepper

1 Bring a pot of salted water to the boil. Discard the heads and rinse the tails of the prawns, then place in the boiling water and simmer for 4–5 minutes. Remove from the water and release the succulent flesh from each shell. Devein them using the tip of a sharp knife to remove any dark thread (the intestine) you see there. Set aside and cover to keep warm.

2 While lightly toasting the bread under a grill, heat the butter in a frying pan and lightly fry the eggs over a medium heat, seasoning with salt and pepper.

3 Butter the toasted bread, add the cooked prawns, top with a fried egg, season with more pepper and serve garnished with rocket leaves and drizzled with extra virgin olive oil.

IF YOU CAN'T GET FRESH DUBLIN BAY PRAWNS (LANGOUSTINES), THEN SOME GOOD-SIZED ATLANTIC OR TIGER PRAWNS WOULD BE GOOD SUBSTITUTES.

Courgette, Tomato and Goat's Cheese Quiche

Serves 4

2 courgettes, sliced diagonally to 1cm thick

1 tbsp olive oil

salt and freshly cracked pepper

100g cherry tomatoes, sliced in half

100g goat's cheese, crumbled

2–3 spring onions, sliced

15g basil, leaves only (reserve a few for the garnish)

250ml cream

3 large free-range eggs, lightly whisked

SHORTCRUST PASTRY

170g plain flour, sieved

100g butter, cubed small (chilled)

pinch of salt

1–2 tbsp cold water

Preheat the oven to 200°C/400°F/gas mark 6.

1 To make the pastry, put the flour, butter and salt in a food processor and pulse until the fat and flour are combined to a breadcrumb consistency (this can also be done by hand). With the motor running, gradually add the water through the funnel until the dough comes together (add just enough water to bind it). Wrap the dough in cling film and chill for 20 minutes before rolling out on a lightly floured work surface. Place in a 20cm loose-bottomed flan tin, prick the pastry with a fork and bake blind. (Line the pastry with parchment paper, fill with baking beans and place in the oven for 25 minutes, until the base is crisp and golden. Remove the beans and paper.)

2 Heat the oil in a heavy-bottomed frying pan and fry the courgettes until lightly golden on each side. Season well.

3 In 2 layers, arrange the courgettes, tomatoes (cut side facing upwards), goat's cheese, spring onions and basil leaves in the cooked pastry case. Season well. Repeat with a second layer, finishing with a layer of tomatoes.

4 Whisk together the cream and eggs and season well.

5 Slowly pour the egg mixture over the filling, giving it time to seep through the gaps (if you pour it in too quickly, it might spill over the sides of the tin).

6 Place the quiche on a baking sheet in the oven and bake for 35–40 minutes, until golden and risen in the centre.

7 Remove from the oven and scatter with the remaining basil leaves. Leave to sit for 10 minutes before serving. Serve with a salad of mixed leaves with asparagus and pine nuts (see p. 59).

Asparagus Tart

Serves 4

During week 1 of our Professional Certificate course, our students make a variety of delicious quiches and tarts and hone their skills by learning how to bake pastry blind.

250g asparagus spears, woody ends snapped off

3 large free-range eggs, lightly whisked

250ml cream

50g mature white cheddar cheese, grated

salt and freshly cracked black pepper

SHORTCRUST PASTRY

170g plain flour, sieved

100g butter, cubed small (chilled)

pinch of salt

1–2 tbsp cold water

Pre-heat the oven to 180°C/350°F/gas mark 4.

1 To make the pastry, put the flour, butter and salt in a food processor and pulse until combined to a breadcrumb consistency (this can also be done by hand). With the motor running, gradually add the water through the funnel until the dough comes together (add just enough water to bind it). Wrap the dough in cling film and chill for 20 minutes before rolling out on a lightly floured work surface. Place in a 20cm loose-bottomed flan tin, prick the pastry with a fork and bake blind (line the pastry with parchment paper, fill with baking beans and place in the oven for 25 minutes, until the base is crisp and golden. Remove the beans and paper).

2 Reserve 6 asparagus spears, each long enough to fit from the centre of the tin to the outer edge, for later use. Chop the remaining spears into 4cm lengths and place them over the cooked pastry base.

3 Whisk the eggs and cream together and season well with salt and pepper. Pour this mixture over the asparagus before scattering the grated cheese evenly over the filled tart. Arrange the reserved spears in a fan pattern (or concentrically) over the top of the tart, with the tips pointing outwards.

4 Place the tart on a baking sheet in the oven and bake for 35 minutes, until risen and slightly golden.

5 Leave to sit for 10 minutes before serving. Serve with a green salad (see p. 42).

Aubergine and Goat's Cheese Stacks

Serves 4

These stacks can be prepared in advance and quickly warmed through in the oven before serving. Mozzarella, feta or Parmesan cheese can all be substituted for the goat's cheese.

2 medium aubergines

150g goat's cheese, crumbled

10g fresh basil, leaves only

TOMATO SAUCE

1 onion, finely chopped

2 tbsp olive oil (and more for brushing over aubergine slices)

2 cloves garlic, crushed

1 x 400g tin chopped tomatoes

1 tsp sugar

1 tbsp balsamic vinegar (or red wine vinegar)

salt and freshly cracked black pepper

Preheat the oven to 190°C/375°F/gas mark 5.

1 For the sauce, sweat the onion in olive oil over a gentle heat for 10 minutes, until translucent. Add the garlic and cook for a few seconds. Increase the heat and add the tomatoes, sugar, balsamic vinegar and seasoning. Allow to simmer uncovered for 20 minutes until reduced by half, stirring occasionally.

2 Meanwhile, top and tail each aubergine and slice into 1cm-thick round discs. Brush each round on both sides with olive oil and place on a baking tray in the oven for 20 minutes, until softened and slightly golden underneath.

3 Once the sauce and aubergines are ready, start layering. Take the largest round, spread tomato sauce over it, then some crumbled goat's cheese, followed by a few basil leaves. Repeat the layers, finishing with a slice of aubergine. Serve warm.

Vegetable Samosas

Serves 4

This classic Indian street food makes perfect party nibbles. At Cooks Academy, we bake the samosas rather than deep frying them, as we find this method is healthier and handier.

$^1/_2$ tsp fennel seeds

$^1/_2$ tsp coriander seeds

1 tsp cumin seeds

1 tsp garam masala

$^1/_2$ tsp chilli powder

$^1/_2$ tsp turmeric

1 tbsp olive oil

1 small onion, finely chopped

2 garlic cloves, finely chopped

2cm fresh ginger, peeled and finely chopped

2 carrots, finely diced

1 sweet potato, diced small

75g frozen peas, defrosted

10g fresh coriander, leaves chopped

200g filo pastry sheets, defrosted

Preheat the oven to 180°C/350°F/gas mark 4.

1 Gently heat the fennel, coriander and cumin seeds in a small heavy-based frying pan for 1 minute (ensure the spices do not burn). Transfer to a pestle and mortar and grind the spices well before adding in the garam masala, chilli powder, turmeric and 1 tbsp water.

2 Heat the olive oil in a frying pan and gently fry the onion, garlic and ginger for 2 minutes. Stir in 1 tbsp of the spice paste, the carrots and sweet potato along with 4 tbsp water and cook until the vegetables are al dente, adding more water if the mixture dries out. Remove from the pan and allow to cool before adding in the peas and chopped coriander leaves.

3 Cut the filo pastry sheets into 9cm x 30cm strips. To make the triangular samosas, place 2 teaspoonfuls of the filling in the lowest right-hand corner of each strip and fold the corner over diagonally to form a triangle, continuing on from the opposite corner until you reach the top of each strip. Repeat and lightly brush each triangle with olive oil before transferring to a baking sheet and baking in the oven for 20 minutes, until crisp and golden.

4 Serve as a starter with mango salsa (see p. 145) and a mint raita (see p. 198) or serve as party nibbles with mango chutney.

Tian of Crab with Avocado and Melon

Serves 4

This combination of tastes is sublime. However, if you don't have crabmeat, some chicken would also be delicious.

200g fresh cooked crabmeat

1 tbsp crème fraîche

2 tsp lemon juice

1 tsp Dijon mustard

1 avocado

3 tsp extra virgin olive oil

1 tsp white wine vinegar

1 tsp honey

100g mixed lettuce leaves, washed

100g Galia melon, cut into chunks

15g sunflower seeds, lightly toasted, to serve

salt and freshly cracked black pepper

1 Pick through the crabmeat, removing any pieces of shell. Gently squeeze out and discard any excess liquid and place in a bowl (the resulting consistency should be sticky). Stir in the crème fraîche, half the lemon juice and the mustard. Season well.

2 Peel and very finely dice the avocado and stir in the remaining lemon juice to stop the flesh discolouring. Season.

3 Press the crab mixture into the bottom of 4 ramekins (first, lightly grease each ramekin with unscented oil), then follow with a layer of avocado. Refrigerate for at least 30 minutes, removing from the fridge 10 minutes before serving.

4 Mix together the olive oil, vinegar and honey and season. Toss the mixed leaves through the dressing and add the melon. Divide the salad between 4 starter plates.

5 Upend the ramekins onto the centre of the dressed lettuce leaves. Use the tip of a sharp knife to coax the tians out. Sprinkle with sunflower seeds and serve.

....

TO PEEL AN AVOCADO: CUT IN HALF LENGTHWAYS AND TWIST THE HALVES IN OPPOSITE DIRECTIONS. CAREFULLY REMOVE THE STONE. WITH EACH HALF FACE DOWN ON A BOARD, LIGHTLY CUT ALONG THE LENGTH AND CAREFULLY PEEL THE SKIN BACKWARDS.

Rosti with Smoked Salmon, Capers and Chives

Serves 4

This starter goes down a treat on Christmas Day. For a little drama or a special occasion, add the lumpfish roe or even caviar!

2 large baking potatoes, washed

300g smoked salmon, sliced

1 shallot, finely chopped

2 tsp baby capers

3 tbsp chopped chives

4 tbsp crème fraîche

50ml extra virgin olive oil

2 tbsp olive oil, for frying

4 tsp lumpfish roe (optional)

salt and freshly cracked black pepper

Preheat the oven to 200°C/400°F/gas mark 6.

1 Pierce each potato deeply a few times with a fork or skewer. Bake the potatoes in their skins for 40 minutes (the flesh should not be too soft) and leave to cool.

2 Trim the sliced smoked salmon of any waxy edges and cut into wide ribbons before combining with the shallot and capers.

3 Fold half the chives through the crème fraîche. Season with black pepper.

4 Liquidise the extra virgin olive oil and remaining chives and strain through a sieve.

5 Scoop the potatoes from their skins, coarsely grate and press into 4 round cake shapes (8cm wide). Heat 2 tbsp olive oil in a non-stick frying pan and fry the rosti until golden brown on each side. Set aside and keep warm.

6 Serve the warm rosti topped with smoked salmon, crème fraîche and lumpfish roe (if you have it!) and drizzle over some of the chive oil.

Fig Galette

Serves 4

We include these stylish galettes in our Quick Entertaining course. Once you learn how to make pastry galettes, there is no end to the wonderful toppings you can dream up to serve them with.

200g all-butter puff pastry, defrosted

6 fresh figs

60g caster sugar

2 tsp balsamic vinegar

100g Camembert cheese, cut into 8 slices

fresh chives or basil leaves, to garnish

Preheat the oven to 200°C/400°F/gas mark 6.

1 To make puff pastry galette: If not already pre-rolled, roll out the pastry to 2mm thick and cut out 4 discs using a 10cm wide pastry cutter (or wineglass rim or saucer base). Prick well with a fork and place on a baking sheet lined with a sheet of parchment paper. Cover with a second sheet of parchment paper and weigh down with a second baking tray. Bake for 12 minutes, until crisp and golden.

2 To make the fig jam, chop 3 of the figs into small pieces and place in a saucepan with the sugar and balsamic vinegar. Stir over a low heat until the sugar dissolves, then stop stirring and allow to simmer for 10 minutes. The jam will thicken slightly once it is removed from the heat and as it cools.

3 To assemble the galette, slice each of the remaining figs into 4–6 wedges. Smear a spoonful of jam over each galette and lay 2 slices of camembert in the centre, followed by some fig wedges. To serve, warm in the oven until the cheese just starts to melt. Garnish with fresh herbs.

FOR ENTERTAINING: THE GALETTES CAN BE MADE IN ADVANCE AND STORED IN AN AIRTIGHT CONTAINER FOR 2-3 DAYS.

Salmon Potato Cakes

Serves 4

500g potatoes, peeled and cut in half

25g butter

2 tbsp horseradish sauce

25ml milk, heated

500g salmon, skinned and pin boned

250ml white wine

2–3 fresh dill stalks (reserve leaves)

1 lemon, half juiced, half cut into slices

1 tbsp freshly chopped chives

150g breadcrumbs, seasoned

1 egg, lightly whisked

1–2 tbsp sunflower oil, for frying

100ml double cream (optional)

2 tomatoes, deseeded and diced

salt and freshly cracked black pepper

Preheat the oven to 180°C/350°F/gas mark 4.

1 Steam the potatoes for 15–20 minutes or until they can be pierced easily with a fork. Mash with the butter and horseradish sauce, adding the hot milk towards the end. Set aside in a large bowl, cover and keep warm.

2 Place the salmon in a baking tray. Add the wine, dill stalks and lemon slices and season. Cover with tin foil and bake in the oven for 15 minutes, until the fish starts to flake when tested with a knife. Reserve the cooking liquid by straining the fish through a sieve (leave the fish to sit for a few minutes in the sieve to catch any additional juice).

3 Gently mix the strained salmon, dill leaves and chives into the bowl of warm mash. Season well. Shape the mixture into 4 large cakes (alternatively, you could shape into 12 small cakes).

4 With the breadcrumbs on a dinner plate and the egg in a bowl, quickly dip each cake into the egg before rolling it in the breadcrumbs. Over a medium-high heat, fry the cakes in the sunflower oil until golden and crisp. Set aside and keep warm.

5 Simmer the reserved cooking liquid in a pan until reduced by half. Add the cream and continue boiling until further reduced and thickened. Stir in the tomatoes and add the lemon juice, to taste.

6 Quickly reheat the fish cakes in the oven and serve with the sauce and a green salad (see p. 42).

The People's Park, Dún Laoghaire

Quinoa Stack with Mediterranean Vegetables

Serves 4

A light, healthy and colourful starter for a summer's day.

150g quinoa

400ml vegetable stock

salt and freshly cracked pepper

1 x 300g courgette, sliced into
  1cm rings

1 red pepper, deseeded and
  roughly chopped

1 yellow pepper, deseeded and
  roughly chopped

1 red onion, peeled and cut into
  large cubes

2 cloves garlic, crushed

2 tbsp olive oil

15g fresh rocket, to serve

15g Parmesan shavings, to
  serve

DRESSING

2 tbsp extra virgin olive oil

1 tbsp balsamic vinegar

1 tsp honey, to taste

Preheat the oven to 170°C/325°F/gas mark 3.

1 Rinse the quinoa using a sieve, rubbing your fingers through the grains until the water runs clear. Place the quinoa in a saucepan and add the stock. Cover with a lid and bring to the boil, then simmer for 12–15 minutes, until all the liquid is absorbed, stirring occasionally. Drizzle a dash of olive oil through the quinoa and lightly season. Set aside and keep warm.

2 Mix together the courgette, peppers, red onion and garlic. Drizzle with olive oil and season. Transfer to a baking sheet and roast in the oven for 30 minutes, stirring once or twice to stop the onions burning. When the peppers are soft to the touch, remove all the vegetables from the oven and set aside.

3 Just before serving, combine the dressing ingredients and add just enough to the rocket leaves to coat them lightly. Place a handful of rocket leaves in the centre of each serving plate.

4 Place a metal ring over the leaves and half fill the ring with quinoa, packing the grains tightly. Finish with a layer of roasted vegetables. Carefully remove the metal ring. Lastly, sprinkle Parmesan shavings over the top.

QUINOA IS CORRECTLY PRONOUNCED 'KEEN-WHAH'

CHAPTER 3 Salads

Green Salad with a Classic French Dressing

Serves 4

150g mixed green lettuce
  (butterhead, frisée), washed

10g flat leaf parsley, leaves
  picked

FRENCH DRESSING

1 tbsp white wine vinegar

6 tbsp good-quality extra virgin
  olive oil

$^{1}/_{2}$ tsp Dijon mustard

1 tsp honey

sea salt and freshly cracked
  black pepper

1 In a large bowl, mix together the washed lettuce and parsley leaves (dry the leaves thoroughly so the dressing clings to the leaves when tossed).

2 Whisk the dressing ingredients until emulsified. Season to taste.

3 Just before serving, toss the salad in enough dressing to lightly coat the leaves. Store any remaining dressing in the fridge for up to 2 weeks.

ADD LEFTOVER FRESH HERBS TO THIS SALAD FOR A REAL
BURST OF FLAVOUR.

Mixed Leaves with Peppers and a Honey Mustard Dressing

Serves 4

¹/₂ cucumber

150g mixed lettuce leaves, washed (e.g. oak leaf, lollo rosso, frisée)

¹/₂ red pepper, deseeded and finely sliced lengthways

¹/₂ yellow pepper, deseeded and finely sliced lengthways

¹/₂ red onion, peeled and cut into very finely sliced wedges

HONEY MUSTARD DRESSING

3 tbsp good-quality extra virgin olive oil

2 tbsp lemon juice

1 tsp Dijon mustard

2 tsp honey

1 clove garlic, peeled

sea salt and freshly cracked black pepper

1 Whisk all the dressing ingredients (except the garlic) together, adjusting the sweetness to your taste by adding more honey, if required. Add the garlic clove.

2 Cut the cucumber in half lengthways, then cut each half again. Align the 4 pieces alongside each other and slice across into small triangles.

3 Place the lettuce leaves in a bowl and add all the prepared salad ingredients.

4 Just before serving, remove the clove of garlic from the dressing and toss the dressing through the salad.

TO FRESHEN UP LETTUCE, ALWAYS WASH THE LEAVES IN ICY COLD WATER. BE GENTLE WHEN WASHING LETTUCE, AS THE LEAVES ARE DELICATE AND BRUISE EASILY.

Roasted Beetroot, Feta and Radish Salad

Serves 4

When you buy beetroot at a farmers' market, the attractive pink-veined leaves are usually attached. Leave a few centimetres of stalk attached to the beetroot, wash the tender leaves and add them to the salad.

12 small (or 6 medium) beetroots, skins scrubbed clean

1 tbsp olive oil

1 tbsp balsamic vinegar

100g batavia lettuce (or mixed leaves)

6 radishes, quartered

100g feta cheese, lightly crumbled

DRESSING

2 tbsp extra virgin olive oil

1 tbsp walnut oil

1 tbsp balsamic vinegar

1 tsp lemon juice

$^1/_2$ tsp honey

1 tsp wholegrain mustard

sea salt and freshly cracked black pepper

Preheat the oven to 200°C/400°F/gas mark 6.

1 Coat the beetroot lightly in olive oil. Wrap the beetroot in pairs in tin foil and roast in the oven for 45 minutes, until slightly softened (medium or large beetroots will need longer). Remove from the oven, top and tail the beetroots and cut each into quarters.

2 Drizzle the beetroot with balsamic vinegar. Return the beetroot quarters to the oven, turn down the oven to 180°C/350°F/gas mark 4 and roast for another 15 minutes, or until the edges are starting to caramelise.

3 Meanwhile, whisk together the dressing ingredients. Toss half the dressing through the mixed salad leaves to coat lightly.

4 To serve, divide the mixed leaves between plates. Arrange the radishes, beetroot and feta over the bed of lettuce and drizzle with any remaining dressing.

WALNUT AND HAZELNUT OILS HAVE A NUTTY FLAVOUR WHICH IS QUITE STRONG, SO THEY ARE USUALLY MIXED WITH OLIVE OIL.

Carrot Salad

Serves 4

2 tbsp raisins

5 organic carrots, peeled

RED WINE VINAIGRETTE

3 tbsp good-quality extra virgin
  olive oil

2 tbsp red wine vinegar

salt and freshly cracked black
  pepper

1 Whisk together the vinaigrette ingredients and season to taste.

2 Soak the raisins in 2 tbsp of the dressing for 15 minutes.

3 Using the grating attachment of a food processor, grate the carrot as finely as possible. Season well with salt and pepper.

4 Stir the raisins through the carrots and add more dressing as required. Chill before serving.

WHEN MAKING A GRATED CARROT SALAD, IT IS REALLY
WORTH USING ORGANIC CARROTS, AS THEY HAVE A
LOWER WATER CONTENT BUT TONS MORE FLAVOUR.

Julienne Salad of Carrot, Cucumber and Mint

Serves 4

This fresh Asian salad is inspired by our superb tutor Gráinne Wall and goes with just about everything.

1 cucumber, skin on, seeded and
  julienned (sliced into thin
  matchsticks)

3 medium carrots, julienned

5g fresh coriander, leaves only

5g fresh mint, leaves only

RICE WINE DRESSING

60ml rice vinegar

25g caster sugar

$1/2$ red chilli, deseeded and finely
  chopped

1 garlic clove, finely chopped

1 To make the dressing, heat the vinegar and sugar in a small non-reactive saucepan. Add the chilli and garlic and stir until the sugar is dissolved. Remove from the heat and allow to cool.

2 In a large bowl, toss the julienned vegetables through the dressing along with the coriander leaves. Refrigerate.

3 Just before serving, roughly chop the mint leaves and stir them through the salad.

TO JULIENNE VEGETABLES, CUT THEM INTO MATCH-
STICK-THIN SLICES.

Smoked Chicken and Grape Salad

Serves 4

Cooked chicken or smoked duck breasts could be used just as well in this salad, which doubles up as a stylish starter.

50g walnuts, halved

2 smoked chicken breasts (or use cooked chicken breasts, see note below)

200g rocket leaves

2 sprigs flat leaf parsley, leaves only (or chervil)

100g red seedless grapes, washed and halved

2 ruby grapefruit, peeled and segmented

WALNUT DRESSING

1 clove garlic, crushed

$^{1}/_{2}$ tsp wholegrain mustard

2 tbsp olive oil

1 tbsp walnut oil

1 tbsp white wine vinegar

sea salt and freshly cracked black pepper

Preheat the oven to 180°C/350°F/gas mark 4.

1 Place the walnuts on a baking sheet and roast in the oven for 5 minutes to toast lightly. Set aside to cool.

2 Slice the smoked chicken breasts diagonally into 2mm-thin slices.

3 Whisk together the dressing ingredients until fully emulsified. Season to taste.

4 Just before serving, toss the rocket, parsley and grapes with the dressing in a large bowl. Transfer to a serving platter and scatter over the sliced chicken and walnuts. Serve immediately, garnished with grapefruit segments.

....

TO COOK CHICKEN BREASTS, PLACE ON A BAKING SHEET AND DRIZZLE WITH OLIVE OIL AND SEASON WITH SALT AND PEPPER. COOK IN AN OVEN PREHEATED TO 180°C/350°F/GAS MARK 4 FOR 15 MINUTES, UNTIL COOKED THROUGH.

Tuscan Bread Salad

Serves 4

Our corporate team-building events are marvellous bonding occasions for work colleagues. This recipe is used in our Italian-themed event. Like most Italian recipes, once the preparation is done, it's really easy to put together this satisfying salad. It's ideal for a quick summer meal.

2 tbsp pine nuts

2 red peppers, deseeded and quartered

2 yellow peppers, deseeded and quartered

2 tbsp olive oil

2 cloves garlic, crushed

100g ciabatta bread, roughly torn into chunks

6 vine tomatoes, cut into chunks (or eighths)

3 tbsp pitted Kalamata olives, halved

2 tbsp baby capers

5g basil leaves, torn

DRESSING

6 tbsp good-quality extra virgin olive oil

1 tbsp balsamic vinegar

$^1\!/_2$ tsp honey

salt and freshly cracked black pepper

Preheat the oven to 180°C/350°F/gas mark 4.

1 Roast the pine nuts on a baking sheet for 6 minutes, until golden brown. Allow to cool.

2 Preheat the grill to hot. Place the peppers on a baking sheet skin side up and grill until blackened and blistered (this might take anything from 5 to 15 minutes). Place in a bowl and cover immediately with cling film and leave for 20 minutes to cool (the cling film will trap the steam and loosen the skins). Once the skins have loosened, peel the peppers and discard the skin.

3 Mix the olive oil and garlic together in a small bowl. Place the chunks of bread on a baking sheet and drizzle with the strained garlic-infused oil (reserve the bowl to make the dressing). Season and bake in the oven for 10 minutes, until golden brown. Keep warm.

4 In a large salad bowl, combine the peppers, tomatoes, olives, capers and toasted pine nuts.

5 Whisk together the dressing ingredients until emulsified and season to taste. Just before serving, toss the dressing through the salad and add the ciabatta and basil leaves.

SKINNING PEPPERS LIKE THIS IS THE IDEAL WAY TO REMOVE THE SKINS, WHICH SOME PEOPLE FIND INDIGESTIBLE. YOU CAN ALSO REMOVE THEM FROM THE RAW PEPPER WITH A WIDE VEGETABLE PEELER.

Watercress Salad with Blue Cheese and Honeyed Pecans

Serves 4

50g pecan nuts

2 tbsp honey

1 ripe pear, thinly sliced

150g blue cheese (St Agur, Cashel Blue or Stilton), chilled

150g watercress, washed

2 tsp chives, finely chopped

DRESSING

4 tbsp good-quality extra virgin olive oil

3 tbsp lemon juice

1 tbsp honey

1 clove garlic, crushed

salt and freshly cracked black pepper

Preheat the oven to 180°C/350°F/gas mark 4.

1 Place the pecans in an ovenproof dish or baking tray and drizzle with the honey. Place in the oven for 8–10 minutes, until the honey darkens and bubbles (stir halfway through to recoat the nuts as the honey loosens).

2 Mix together the dressing ingredients and season to taste.

3 Slice the pear (if preparing ahead, toss in lemon juice to prevent the pear from discolouring).

4 Remove the cheese from the fridge and crumble into small pieces.

5 Just before serving, place the watercress in a salad bowl and toss in the dressing until the leaves are evenly coated.

6 Scatter over the honeyed nuts, blue cheese, pear, and chives. Serve immediately.

ONCE CARAMELISED, KEEP THE PECANS FROM STICKING TOGETHER BY PLACING THEM ON A PLATE BRUSHED LIGHTLY WITH UNSCENTED OIL. THIS KEEPS THE PECANS FROM STICKING TOGETHER AND MAKES THEM EASIER TO TOSS INTO A SALAD.

French Bean Salad

Serves 4

A French bean salad can be served warm or cold, depending on the time of year. Both methods are given here.

200g French beans, tips trimmed

1 clove garlic, crushed

RED WINE VINAIGRETTE

3 tbsp good-quality extra virgin olive oil

1 tbsp red wine vinegar

1 tsp honey

1 tbsp freshly chopped flat leaf parsley

salt and freshly cracked black pepper

1 Bring a saucepan of water to the boil, adding a generous dessertspoon of salt. Trim the top ends of the French beans, then add to the boiling water. Simmer for 2–3 minutes, until the beans are cooked but with a slight bite (al dente).

2 **For a warm salad without dressing:** Strain the beans and shake well to remove all the water. While the beans are still hot, stir in the garlic, a generous grinding of cracked black pepper and drizzle with olive oil. Serve warm or at room temperature.

3 **For a cold salad:** Once cooked, remove the beans from the water and immediately immerse in cold water (this arrests the cooking process so the beans retain their vibrant green colour). Drain and pat the beans dry with kitchen paper, then toss the beans in the dressing.

4 Make the dressing by whisking together the extra virgin olive oil, vinegar and honey. Season to taste. Stir in the chopped parsley, toss the beans in the dressing and serve.

Crisp Chicken Salad with Coconut Milk Dressing

Serves 4

This fabulous creamy dressing is well worth making. Refrigerate any leftover coconut milk and use it to make the Thai red monkfish curry (p. 128) a few days later.

3–4 chicken breasts, with skin on (or leftover cooked chicken)

4 shallots, skinned and thinly sliced

2 cloves of garlic, skinned and halved

3 tbsp olive oil

1 cucumber, halved lengthways and deseeded

1 red pepper, deseeded and cut into thin strips

2 red chillies, deseeded and finely chopped

10g mint, leaves only (roughly chop any large leaves)

150g crisp green lettuce (iceberg, romaine or baby gem)

freshly cracked black pepper

COCONUT MILK DRESSING

3 tbsp lime juice

2 tbsp coconut milk

1/2–1 tbsp fish sauce

1 tbsp sweet chilli sauce

Preheat the oven to 190°C/375°F/gas mark 5.

1 To cook the chicken, place the chicken (skin side up), shallots and garlic on a roasting tray lined with baking parchment. Drizzle with olive oil and season. Cook in the preheated oven for 30 minutes, until the chicken is cooked through. Set aside to cool.

2 Slice the cucumber thinly into half moons. Discard the skin from the chicken and shred the meat into thin pieces.

3 Gently toss the shredded chicken, crisp shallots (discard any burnt ones), cucumber, red pepper, chilli and half the mint leaves in a bowl (reserve the smallest leaves as a garnish). Arrange over a bed of crisp lettuce leaves.

4 Combine the dressing ingredients (adjusting the flavours according to your taste) and whisk well.

5 Just before serving, pour the dressing over the salad and garnish with the remaining mint leaves.

DESEEDING THE CUCUMBER REMOVES THE EXCESS MOISTURE IN THE CUCUMBER. SCRAPE OUT THE SEEDS USING THE TIP OF A TEASPOON.

Salad Niçoise

Serves 4

This salad is perfect for a summer evening meal, arranged on individual plates before serving.

200g baby potatoes, halved

4 eggs, at room temperature

200g French beans, topped and tailed

1 medium cos or romaine lettuce, leaves torn into chunks

2 x 200g tins tuna fish, well drained

250g cherry tomatoes, halved

1 spring onion, thinly sliced

50g pitted black olives, halved

6–8 anchovy fillets, drained

DRESSING

1 tbsp white wine vinegar

6 tbsp good-quality extra virgin olive oil

1/2 tsp Dijon mustard

1 tsp honey

1 clove garlic, crushed

sea salt and freshly cracked black pepper

1 For the potatoes, bring a medium saucepan of water to the boil and add 1 tbsp table salt. Add the potatoes and boil for 15 minutes (always test one potato before draining the water from the saucepan). Drain in a colander and leave for 10 minutes while the steam rises off the potatoes.

2 For the eggs, bring a small saucepan of water to the boil, add a little table salt, then lower the eggs gently into the water with a spoon (the eggs should be covered in water). Return to the boil, then simmer gently for 7 minutes for a soft yolk and a solid white. Immerse the cooked eggs in cold water to cool completely, then remove the shell and cut into quarters.

3 For the French beans, bring a saucepan of water to the boil, adding a generous dessertspoon of salt. Add the beans to the boiling water and simmer for 2–3 minutes, until the beans are cooked but with a slight bite (al dente). Remove from the water and immediately immerse in ice-cold water (this arrests the cooking process so the beans retain their vibrant green colour).

4 Whisk the dressing ingredients together and season to taste.

5 Divide the torn lettuce leaves between 4 plates. Break the tuna into chunky flakes and place in the centre of the leaves and drizzle half the dressing over. Arrange the potatoes, French beans, tomatoes, spring onion and olives over the salad, followed by the quartered eggs. Finally, garnish with a few anchovy fillets and drizzle over the remaining dressing. Serve immediately.

....

TO TEST IF AN EGG IS FRESH, PLACE IT IN A BOWL OF WATER. IF IT SINKS TO THE BOTTOM, IT'S FRESH; IF IT FLOATS TO THE TOP, IT'S NOT.

Tuna and Green Pepper Salad

Serves 4

This makes a lovely sandwich filling or a light lunch with warm crusty bread. Good-quality tuna and extra virgin olive oil make all the difference. You could add a little mayo for extra creaminess, or add butter beans for a buffet salad.

2 x 200g good-quality tinned tuna in oil

1 green pepper, deseeded and finely diced

½ small red onion, finely chopped

2 tbsp chopped flat leaf parsley

DRESSING

4 tbsp good-quality extra virgin olive oil

1-1½ tbsp sherry vinegar

1 tbsp lemon juice

salt and freshly cracked black pepper

1 Drain the tuna of oil, place in a bowl and flake with a fork.

2 Mix together the dressing ingredients until emulsified, and season. Stir the dressing into the flaked tuna.

3 Lastly, stir in the green pepper, red onion and parsley. Adjust seasoning to taste.

Potato Salad with Maple Syrup Dressing

Serves 4

This non-mayonnaise salad was inspired by Thyme Out, Dalkey. It's so quick and easy. If you don't have time to make the dressing ingredients, stir crème fraîche through the warm potatoes and garnish with a few pink peppercorns.

100g smoked pancetta slices, cut into small squares

500g baby potatoes, cut in half or quarters

5 spring onions, thinly sliced

5g flat leaf parsley, leaves only

MAPLE SYRUP DRESSING

1 clove garlic, crushed

1/2 tsp wholegrain mustard

1 tsp maple syrup

1 tbsp white wine vinegar

4 tbsp extra virgin olive oil

sea salt and freshly cracked black pepper

Preheat the oven to 180°C/350°F/gas mark 4.

1 Whisk together the dressing ingredients until emulsified and season to taste.

2 Place the pancetta on a baking sheet and bake in the oven for 8–10 minutes, until lightly crisp. Transfer to a plate lined with kitchen paper to remove any excess oil.

3 Bring a large saucepan of water to the boil and add 1 tbsp table salt. Add the potatoes and simmer for 12–15 minutes, until cooked (test one potato before draining the water from the saucepan). Drain in a colander and leave for 10 minutes while the steam rises off the potatoes.

4 While still warm, transfer the potatoes to a wide bowl and toss in the dressing. Stir in the crisp pancetta, spring onions and parsley. Season well. Serve warm or chilled.

....

BOTH DIJON AND WHOLEGRAIN MUSTARDS WORK WELL IN DRESSINGS, AS THEY ARE MUCH MILDER THAN ENGLISH MUSTARD.

Tangy Melon Salad

Serves 4

Vibrant and refreshing, this salad makes a perfect starter to offset a rich main course.

15g sunflower seeds

1 ripe cantaloupe melon, cut into bite-sized chunks

8–10 (100g) radishes, finely sliced

10g fresh coriander, leaves only

1 sprig fresh mint, leaves only (roughly tear any large leaves)

100g feta cheese, cut into cubes

DRESSING

2 tsp fresh root ginger, peeled and grated

$^{1}/_{2}$ green chilli, deseeded and finely chopped

1 tbsp light soy sauce

4 tbsp olive oil

$^{1}/_{2}$ tsp toasted sesame oil

1 tbsp lime juice, or to taste

sea salt and freshly cracked black pepper

Preheat the oven to 180°C/350°F/gas mark 4.

1 Toast the sunflower seeds on a baking sheet in the oven for 5 minutes. Set aside to cool.

2 Whisk the dressing ingredients together in a bowl, adding more or less lime juice to taste. Adjust seasoning (there is no need to adjust the sweetness, as the melon will be added later).

3 Just before serving, place the melon and radishes in a salad bowl and stir through half the dressing. Add the fresh herbs and stir in more dressing, if required. Divide between plates and scatter over the feta and a sprinkling of sunflower seeds.

EXERCISE CAUTION WHEN HANDLING CHILLIES, AS THE JUICES CAN IRRITATE YOUR SKIN. WEAR THIN VINYL GLOVES AND REMEMBER NOT TO RUB YOUR EYES.

Mixed Leaf Salad with Asparagus and Pine Nuts

Serves 4

Another favourite salad featured in our Summer Buffets course. We have added lemon thyme to the dressing, which is gorgeous in salads. Buy a potted lemon thyme plant next time you visit a garden centre and it will last all summer.

50g pine nuts

100g asparagus spears

150g mixed lettuce leaves, washed (frisée, lollo rosso or oak leaf)

1 avocado, peeled, stoned and sliced (or cut into bite-sized chunks)

6–10 cherry tomatoes, halved

75g Parmesan shavings

DRESSING

1 clove garlic, crushed

1 shallot, finely chopped

$^1/_2$ tsp Dijon mustard

40ml red wine vinegar

90ml extra virgin olive oil

$^1/_2$ tsp honey

2 sprigs lemon thyme leaves (if available) or chopped parsley

salt and freshly cracked black pepper

Preheat the oven to 180°C/350°F/gas mark 4.

1 Whisk together the dressing ingredients (except the herbs). Adjust the honey and seasoning to taste before adding the herbs.

2 Meanwhile, roast the pine nuts on a baking tray for 6 minutes, until golden brown. Set aside to cool.

3 Bring a saucepan of water to the boil, adding a generous dessertspoon of salt. Snap off and discard the woody ends of the asparagus and add the spears to the boiling water. Simmer for 4 minutes before immersing in cold water and draining. Pat the asparagus dry before cutting into 2cm lengths.

4 Place the lettuce leaves in a large, wide salad bowl. Add the asparagus, avocado, tomatoes and half the Parmesan shavings. Just before serving, lightly toss the salad in the dressing and scatter over the toasted pine nuts and remaining Parmesan shavings.

CREATE PARMESAN SHAVINGS USING A WIDE VEGETABLE PEELER.

Puy Lentil Salad

Serves 4

This nutritious salad is even better when the flavours are left to infuse for a few hours. Lemon juice has a natural affinity with Puy lentils.

250g Puy lentils, rinsed

500ml vegetable stock

1 bay leaf

3 large tomatoes, skinned, deseeded and diced

1 red pepper, deseeded and diced small

3 stalks celery, diced small

6 spring onions, sliced diagonally

10g flat leaf parsley, leaves roughly chopped

DRESSING

100ml good-quality extra virgin olive oil

2 tbsp lemon juice

1 tbsp red wine vinegar

2 tsp sugar

2 tsp Dijon mustard

1 clove garlic, crushed

sea salt and freshly cracked black pepper

1 Mix together the dressing ingredients until emulsified and season to taste.

2 In a medium saucepan, bring the lentils, vegetable stock and bay leaf to the boil. Reduce the heat and simmer uncovered for 20 minutes, or until the lentils are al dente (not hard). Meanwhile, skim off any foam during cooking.

3 Remove from the heat, discard the bay leaf and drain off any excess liquid.

4 Leave to cool for 10 minutes before adding the dressing, tomatoes, red pepper, celery, spring onions and parsley.

5 Serve warm or chilled. This salad will keep well in the fridge for 2 days.

PEEL AWAY THE STRINGY OUTER SKIN OF THE CELERY USING A VEGETABLE PEELER.

Pasta Salad with Pesto Chicken

Serves 4

For this recipe, you can use basil, rocket or even red pepper pesto.

150g penne pasta

2 chicken breasts

1 tbsp olive oil

200g cherry tomatoes, cut into quarters

2–3 tbsp good-quality pesto (see p. 201)

2 sprigs fresh basil, leaves torn

salt and freshly cracked black pepper

Preheat the oven to 180°C/350°F/gas mark 4.

1 Bring a large pot of generously salted water to the boil. Add the pasta and simmer for 10–12 minutes, until al dente (or cook as per packet instructions). Once cooked, drain the pasta and while still hot, drizzle with a slick of olive oil.

2 Place the chicken breasts on a baking sheet, drizzle with olive oil and season. Cook in the oven for 15–20 minutes, until cooked through. Once cooled, cut each breast into 5–6 slices at an angle.

3 Place the cooked pasta, sliced chicken and tomatoes in a large mixing bowl. Stir in the pesto until all the ingredients are nicely coated.

4 Scatter the torn basil leaves over the salad and serve.

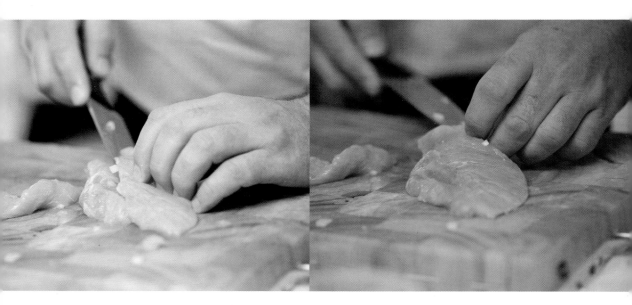

Chickpea Salad with Tomato and Avocado

Serves 4

Students attending our Wholefood courses rave about this deliciously satisfying low GI salad.

4 tomatoes

1 x 400g tin chickpeas, drained and rinsed

¼ red onion, sliced finely into wedges

8 pitted green olives, quartered

½ green chilli, finely chopped

1 red pepper, deseeded and finely chopped

10g fresh basil, leaves roughly torn

2 ripe avocadoes

DRESSING

3 tbsp good-quality extra virgin olive oil

1 tbsp lemon juice

½ tsp honey

2 cloves garlic, crushed

salt and freshly cracked black pepper

1 Whisk together the dressing ingredients until emulsified and season to taste.

2 Remove the stalk from the tomatoes, score a cross in the base of each tomato, then immerse them in boiling water for 30 seconds before plunging into cold water. Peel away the loosened skin and cut the tomatoes into chunks.

3 In a salad bowl, mix together the tomatoes, chickpeas, red onion, olives and chilli and toss to coat in the dressing.

4 Add the red pepper and basil leaves.

5 Just before serving, quarter, stone and peel the avocado. Cut into bite-sized chunks and mix into the salad.

TO SAVE TIME, MIX THE DRESSING INGREDIENTS IN A MIXING BOWL, ADD THE SALAD INGREDIENTS AND TOSS IT ALL TOGETHER JUST BEFORE SERVING.

Quinoa Tabbouleh

Serves 4

Combine any salad vegetables for a variety of colour and to suit your own taste. While tabbouleh often features bulghur wheat or couscous, the nutty flavour of the quinoa grain complements the fresh herbs. While we're at it, we've used a bit of poetic licence by adding some soy sauce, and it works for us.

150g quinoa

400ml water

pinch salt

$^1/_2$ cucumber, skin on, diced small

$^1/_2$ courgette, coarsely grated

2 tomatoes, diced (drain off excess liquid and seeds)

1 red onion, finely diced

25g fresh mint, leaves chopped (or chiffonade)

25g flat leaf parsley, leaves chopped

DRESSING

2 tbsp extra virgin olive oil

1 tbsp lemon juice

1 tbsp soy sauce

pinch paprika

salt and freshly cracked black pepper

1 Rinse the quinoa in a sieve, rubbing your fingers through the grain until the water runs clear.
2 Place the quinoa and water in a saucepan with a pinch of salt. Bring to a boil, cover, then simmer for 15 minutes, stirring occasionally until all the water is absorbed. Set aside to cool (to cool it down quickly, spread it over the surface of a large baking tray, uncovered).
3 When cool, transfer the quinoa to a wide bowl. Stir in the cucumber, courgette, tomatoes, red onion, mint and parsley until fully combined.
4 Next stir through the extra virgin olive oil, lemon juice, soy sauce and paprika. Season to taste. This salad will keep in the fridge for 2 days.

CHIFFONADE MINT BY LAYING THE LEAVES ON TOP OF EACH OTHER, ROLLING THEM INTO A CIGAR SHAPE AND SLICING FINELY.

Spinach, Mango and Chilli Salad

Serves 4

During our Essential Foundation Cookery course most beginner cooks are amazed to see how stunning a salad can be when exotic fruits are added.

50g pine nuts

100g baby asparagus tips

125g baby spinach leaves

1 ripe mango, peeled, stoned and cut into large cubes

1 yellow pepper, deseeded and finely diced

1 red chilli, deseeded and finely chopped

DRESSING

3 tbsp extra virgin olive oil

1 tbsp balsamic vinegar

1 tsp honey

salt and freshly cracked black pepper

Preheat the oven to 180°C/350°F/gas mark 4.

1 Place the pine nuts on a baking sheet and roast in the oven for 6 minutes, until golden brown.

2 Bring a pot of water to the boil. Add a generous dessert-spoon of salt. Add the asparagus to the boiling water and boil for approximately 4 minutes. Remove from the water and immediately immerse in cold water (this arrests the cooking process so the asparagus retains its vibrant green colour). Drain and pat dry.

3 Make the dressing by whisking together the ingredients and season to taste.

4 Arrange the asparagus, spinach, mango and yellow pepper in a large, wide salad bowl or platter.

5 Just before serving, toss lightly in the dressing and scatter over the chilli and toasted pine nuts.

BABY SPINACH LEAVES ARE BEAUTIFULLY TENDER, YET THEY DO NOT WILT AS RAPIDLY AS LETTUCE ONCE A DRESSING IS ADDED.

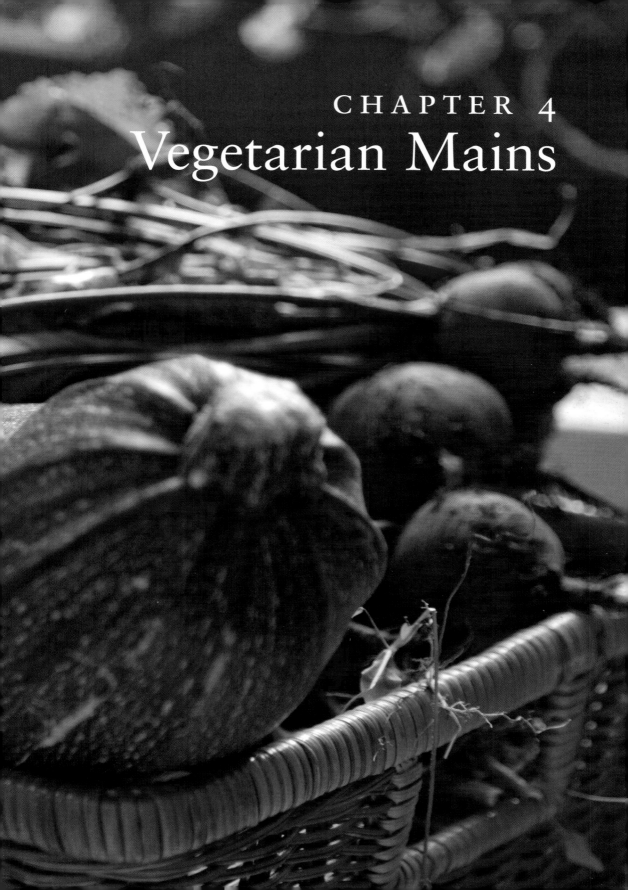

CHAPTER 4
Vegetarian Mains

Cauliflower and Sweet Potato Tagine

Serves 4

A taste of Morocco and a great reason to buy cauliflower! We elevated this noble vegetable by adding this recipe to our Quick Midweek Suppers course and our students always delight in rediscovering its versatility.

2 tbsp olive oil

1 large onion, sliced into thin wedges

2 cloves garlic, crushed

$\frac{1}{2}$ red chilli, deseeded and finely chopped

2 tsp ground cumin

2 tsp ground coriander

1 tsp ground cinnamon

$\frac{1}{2}$ tsp ground turmeric

1 large sweet potato, peeled and chopped into 2cm cubes

300ml vegetable stock

1 x 400g tin chopped tomatoes

2 tbsp honey

$\frac{1}{2}$ lemon, juiced

8 dried ready-to-eat apricots, halved

250g cauliflower, cut into small florets

10g fresh coriander, leaves only

2 tbsp crème fraîche

salt and freshly cracked black pepper

1 Heat the oil in a large non-stick frying pan. Add the onion and sweat for 5 minutes, then add the garlic and chilli and stir for a few minutes before adding in the spices and sweet potato.

2 Stir in the stock, chopped tomatoes, honey, lemon juice and apricots. Season, cover and bring to the boil before simmering over a medium heat for 10 minutes.

3 Add the cauliflower and continue simmering for another 20 minutes. Just before serving, stir in most of the coriander. Serve with couscous, garnished with any remaining coriander leaves and a dollop of crème fraîche.

A POPULAR CONDIMENT IN MOROCCO IS HARISSA, MADE WITH RED CHILLIES, GARLIC, CORIANDER, CUMIN, TURMERIC, CINNAMON AND LEMON. IF YOU CAN BUY THIS FIERY SPICE PASTE, SAVE TIME BY USING IT INSTEAD OF THOSE INGREDIENTS IN THIS RECIPE.

Pancakes with Leeks and Gruyère

Serves 4 (makes 7–8 pancakes)

Use organic eggs for a richer colour and flavour. However, they tend to be smaller, so perhaps use 3. For a darker, nuttier flavour, use buckwheat flour.

120g plain flour

¼ tsp salt

2 large eggs, lightly whisked

200ml milk, mixed together with 75ml cold water

30g butter, melted

1-2 tbsp sunflower oil

1–2 tbsp olive oil and a knob of butter, for frying

5 medium leeks, sliced

1 tbsp Dijon mustard

100g crème fraîche

150g Gruyère cheese, coarsely grated

salt and freshly cracked black pepper

IF YOU DON'T HAVE A CRÊPE PAN, USE A REGULAR SIZE NON-STICK FRYING PAN, WHICH WILL MAKE MUCH LARGER PANCAKES.

Preheat the oven to 160°C/325°F/gas mark 3.

1 Sieve the flour and salt into a large mixing bowl. Make a well in the centre of the flour and crack the eggs into it. Using a whisk, to draw in the flour from around the edges. Gradually add small quantities of the milk and water mixture (any lumps will disappear when whisked vigorously). Stir in the melted butter, then whisk again until the batter is the consistency of pouring cream. Pour the batter into a jug. It can be used immediately.

2 To make the pancakes, add a dash of sunflower oil to a medium-hot non-stick crêpe pan. Pour in 1–2 tbsp of batter, tilting the pan to move the mixture around for a thin and even layer (if you have added too much, tilt the pan and pour off any excess batter back into the jug). Cook each pancake until flecked brown underneath (usually 30 seconds) before flipping onto the other side with a palette knife and cooking for another 30 seconds. Stack the pancakes on a warm plate covered with a cloth in a warm oven.

3 Heat the olive oil and butter in a heavy-based frying pan and lightly sauté the leeks for 2 minutes, seasoning with salt and pepper. Cover with a cartouche (paper lid pressed down onto the leeks; see p. 4) and leave to sweat over a gentle heat until fully softened.

4 Assemble by lightly smearing mustard over each pancake, followed by some leeks (if preparing these in advance, the cooked leeks should be cold for this stage), a spoonful of crème fraîche, then scattering with the grated Gruyère. Roll up and tuck the ends underneath before placing the pancakes side by side on a serving plate. Just before serving, reheat in the oven for 6 minutes. For a more dramatic effect, cut at an angle with a sharp knife and serve 1 half propped over the other.

Pea Risotto

Serves 4

The texture of your risotto should be creamy and oozy with a slight al dente bite. You can always add a bit of butter or cream at the end to achieve this effect if you feel it's a bit too dry.

1 litre vegetable stock, hot (add more if necessary)

50g butter (or 3 tbsp olive oil)

1 onion, finely chopped

200g arborio or carnaroli rice

150ml white wine (or vermouth)

200g petit pois, defrosted

pinch freshly grated nutmeg

10g mint, leaves chopped

20g Parmesan, finely grated

salt and freshly cracked black pepper

1 Heat the stock in a small saucepan and keep hot. In a separate large non-stick pan, gently fry the onion in butter for 6 minutes, until softened.

2 Add the rice and increase the heat, stirring continuously until the grains of rice are evenly coated and turn slightly translucent.

3 Add the wine (or vermouth) and keep stirring (watch that the rice doesn't catch on the bottom of the pan). Once the wine has been absorbed into the rice, add the first ladle of hot stock.

4 Turn down the heat to a brisk simmer so the rice doesn't cook too quickly on the outside. Keep adding ladles of stock, stirring to massage the creamy starch from the rice, allowing each ladle to be absorbed before adding the next (leave one ladleful of stock in the pan to make the pea purée).

5 Using the remaining ladleful of stock in the stock pot, add half the peas and liquidise with a handheld blender to a bright green purée. Season to taste with salt and pepper and a light grating of fresh nutmeg.

6 Stir the rest of the peas through the risotto and heat through before stirring in the purée and mint. Check seasoning, remove from the heat, place a lid on the pan and allow to sit for 2–3 minutes before serving with freshly grated Parmesan.

ADDING THE STOCK WILL TAKE AT LEAST 20 MINUTES AND CANNOT BE RUSHED, AS THE RICE CAN ONLY ABSORB THE LIQUID AT A CERTAIN RATE. THE RISOTTO IS COOKED WHEN THE RICE IS SOFT WHILE STILL RETAINING A SLIGHT BITE.

Grilled Macaroni Cheese

Serves 4

Comfort food – this simple dish is a winner with kids. Our recipe provides for a twist with the juicy cherry tomatoes.

300g cut macaroni (or fusilli or penne)

150g red cheddar, grated

150g cherry tomatoes, quartered

100g breadcrumbs

10g parsley, leaves chopped

WHITE SAUCE

40g butter

40g flour

750ml milk

salt and freshly cracked black pepper

1 Bring a large pot of water to the boil, add a dessertspoon of salt and return to a simmer before adding the pasta and cooking for 10–12 minutes until al dente (or cook as per packet instructions). Once cooked, drain the pasta and keep warm.

2 For the white sauce, melt the butter in a saucepan. Stir in the flour and cook for 1–2 minutes, stirring constantly. Over a medium-high heat, gradually add the milk, stirring constantly. When all the milk is incorporated, lower the heat, add seasoning and simmer gently until the sauce thickens. Remove from the heat and allow to cool slightly. (For a quicker method, make white sauce by putting the milk (cold), butter and flour in a medium pan and cook over a medium heat, whisking until thickened and smooth. Remove from the heat and season.)

3 Add most of the cheese to the sauce (reserve some for the breadcrumbs) and stir until melted.

4 Stir the cheese sauce through the warm pasta and season well with pepper. Add the tomatoes and place in an ovenproof dish (or divide between 4 individual bowls).

5 Mix together the breadcrumbs, chopped parsley and the remaining cheese and sprinkle over the top of the bake. Place under a grill for 5 minutes for a crisp, cheesy crust.

Spinach and Pesto Lasagne

Serves 4

The white sauce in this recipe is made using a quick method, so it's an extremely quick lasagne to make.

500g tender spinach leaves

250g lasagne sheets

3 tbsp good-quality pesto (or see p. 201)

150g fresh mozzarella, sliced

100g fresh Parmesan, grated

10g fresh basil, leaves only (reserve a few for garnishing)

150g cherry tomatoes, halved

salt and freshly cracked black pepper

QUICK WHITE SAUCE

1.2 litres cold milk

75g butter, cubed

75g plain flour

pinch freshly grated nutmeg

Preheat the oven to 180°C/350°F/gas mark 4.

1 For the quick white sauce, put the milk, butter and flour in a saucepan and cook over a medium-high heat, whisking until thickened and smooth. Remove from the heat, season and add the nutmeg to taste.

2 Put the spinach in a colander and pour boiling water over the leaves until wilted down. When cool, squeeze out any excess liquid (alternatively, microwave the spinach for 1 minute, until wilted).

3 Cover the bottom of a 30cm x 2cm ovenproof dish with a thin layer of white sauce and 2–3 non-overlapping sheets of lasagne.

4 While reserving a few basil leaves and grated Parmesan for later, add a third of each ingredient in layers, seasoning well (add layers of white sauce, pesto, spinach, mozzarella, Parmesan, basil leaves, tomatoes (cut side up) and lasagne sheets, in that order). Finish with a layer of lasagne covered in white sauce and the reserved Parmesan cheese (avoid overfilling the dish to prevent leakage).

5 Loosely cover with tin foil and bake for 45 minutes (remove the foil for the last 15 minutes for a golden crust; alternatively, you could place the lasagne uncovered under the grill for 5 minutes). Serve scattered with the reserved basil leaves.

IF YOU RUN OUT OF WHITE SAUCE FOR THE TOP LAYER, MIX IN A BIT OF MILK TO MAKE THE SAUCE GO FURTHER.

Wild Mushroom Pilaf

Serves 4

This pilaf uses pearl barley instead of rice and is given an Asian twist with kecap manis and Chinese five spice seasoning – two great Asian store cupboard essentials.

200g pearl barley (soaked in cold water for 6 hours)

250g mixed wild mushrooms (e.g. shiitake, oyster, chanterelle)

450ml vegetable stock

60ml dry sherry

2 tbsp olive oil

1 onion, finely chopped

2 cloves garlic, crushed

1 tbsp ginger, freshly grated

1 tsp Chinese five spice

200g pak choi, cut into short lengths

1–2 tbsp kecap manis, to taste

1 Rinse the soaked pearl barley well and drain.

2 Wipe all the mushrooms clean and slice thinly.

3 Heat the stock and sherry in a small saucepan, cover and keep at a low simmer.

4 Heat the olive oil in a large non-stick pan over a medium heat. Add the onion and cook for 5 minutes, until softened, then add the garlic, ginger and Chinese five spice and cook for 2 minutes more.

5 Increase the heat and sauté the mushrooms for 2–3 minutes, until lightly golden (but avoid them liquefying).

6 Stir in the pearl barley and hot stock, cover and bring to the boil. Simmer for 35 minutes, until the liquid is absorbed.

7 Lastly, add the kecap manis and stir in the pak choi until it starts to wilt down. Adjust the seasoning to taste and serve.

....

KECAP MANIS IS A SWEET, DARK BROWN SOY SAUCE USED IN INDONESIAN COOKING. CHINESE FIVE SPICE IS A BLEND OF FIVE CLASSIC ASIAN SPICES: STAR ANISE, CINNAMON, FENNEL, CLOVES AND GINGER.

Spinach Wellington

Serves 4

Once you practise the technique of making a savoury plait, you can fill the pastry with all sorts of savoury fillings, like sausage meat or mushrooms. You could also sprinkle some poppy seeds over the pastry to finish. Smoked bacon is delicious added to the spinach if you aren't vegetarian.

500g tender leaf spinach, washed

1 tbsp olive oil

1 onion

200g ricotta cheese (or crumbled feta)

$1/4$ tsp nutmeg, freshly grated

225g ready-rolled puff pastry (rolled into a 20cm x 28cm rectangle)

1 egg, lightly whisked

salt and freshly cracked black pepper

Preheat the oven to 200°C/400°F/gas mark 6.

1 Wash the spinach and with the moisture still clinging to the leaves, wilt in a saucepan (or if bought pre-washed, punch holes in the plastic bag and wilt in the microwave for 2 minutes). Squeeze any excess moisture from the spinach.

2 In a heavy-based frying pan, heat the olive oil and sweat the onion for 10 minutes, until softened.

3 Mix the ricotta and onion through the spinach. Season well with nutmeg, salt and pepper. Set aside to cool (if the filling is hot, it will tear the pastry).

4 Lay the pastry on a sheet of parchment paper placed on a baking sheet. Leaving a 3cm gap at the short ends of the pastry and 6cm on either side, spoon the cooled spinach filling in a mound down the centre, lengthways.

5 From the outer edges of the pastry, cut 2cm-wide strips diagonally inwards, but not actually as far as the central column. To make the plait, fold the top and bottom edges over the filling, then alternately from either side fold each strip in over the filling to create a lattice effect (where the pastry strips meet in the middle, dab with water to seal them together). Lastly, brush egg all over the pastry and bake in the oven for 30 minutes, until the pastry is golden brown and risen.

Lentil Bake

Serves 4

Within the first few months of Cooks Academy opening its doors, Rozanne Stevens joined us as a tutor. She possesses an amazing gift of turning every recipe into a divine dish, while simultaneously wowing her students with her encyclopaedic culinary knowledge.

400g celery, cut into chunks

2 carrots, cut diagonally into chunks

2 tbsp olive oil

590ml vegetable stock

225g brown lentils

1 onion, finely chopped

2 cloves garlic, crushed

2 x 400g tins chopped tomatoes

2 tsp dried oregano

2 sprigs fresh thyme, leaves only

3 sprigs fresh basil, leaves torn

125ml dry red wine

2 tsp honey

30g red cheddar cheese, coarsely grated

50g breadcrumbs

salt and freshly cracked black pepper

WHITE SAUCE
40g butter

3 tbsp plain flour

750ml milk

Preheat the oven to 180°C/350°F/gas mark 4.

1 For the white sauce, melt the butter in a saucepan. Stir in the flour and cook for 1–2 minutes. Over a medium-high heat, gradually add the milk, stirring constantly. When all the milk is incorporated, lower the heat, season and simmer gently, until the sauce thickens. Remove from the heat and allow to cool slightly.

2 Toss the celery and carrots in 1 tbsp olive oil and season well. Place on a baking sheet and bake in the oven for 30–40 minutes, until slightly softened (stir halfway through cooking to ensure the edges don't burn).

3 In a medium saucepan, bring the stock to the boil and add the lentils. Simmer and cook uncovered for 40 minutes, or until tender (rinse the lentils after cooking to remove any cooking foam).

4 Heat 1 tbsp of olive oil in a frying pan and gently sauté the onion for 5 minutes, then add the garlic and continue cooking until soft. Add the tomatoes, herbs, wine and honey and season well. Simmer uncovered for 15 minutes, until thickened, before stirring in the lentils.

5 Pour half the lentil mixture into an ovenproof dish. Layer the roasted vegetables on top, followed by the remaining lentil mixture. Pour the white sauce evenly over the filling, sprinkle over the cheese and lastly cover with the breadcrumbs. Bake uncovered for 40 minutes, until lightly golden, and serve with petit pois or kale.

TO MAKE THIS A COMPLETE MEAL FOR THE FAMILY, SUBSTITUTE MASHED POTATO FOR THE BREADCRUMB TOPPING.

Aubergine and Coconut Curry

Serves 4

Tins of chopped tomatoes, chickpeas and coconut milk make great store cupboard standbys. In combining them, this recipe is a big hit in our Quick Midweek Suppers course!

4 tbsp olive oil

1 medium aubergine, cut into bite-sized chunks

1 medium onion, chopped

2cm piece ginger, peeled and coarsely grated

1 red chilli, chopped

1 tbsp garam masala

1 carrot, peeled and cut into chunks

1 large potato, peeled and cut into chunks

1 x 400g tin chopped tomatoes

1 x 400g tin chickpeas (or butter beans or cannellini beans), drained and rinsed

1 x 400ml tin coconut milk

15g fresh coriander, leaves only

125g tender leaf spinach

salt and freshly cracked black pepper

1 Heat 2 tbsp oil in a large non-stick pan and stir-fry the aubergine until golden brown and beginning to soften. Set aside on a plate.

2 Add another 1 tbsp olive oil to the pan and fry the onion over a medium heat for 10 minutes, until softened.

3 Add the ginger, chilli and garam masala to the onion and stir-fry for 2 minutes.

4 Return the aubergine to the pan along with the carrot, potato, tomatoes, chickpeas and coconut milk. Bring to the boil, cover and simmer gently, until the potato and carrot are just tender, about 15 minutes.

5 Taste and add seasoning. Just before serving, stir the spinach leaves through the curry until wilted, followed by half the coriander leaves. Garnish with the remaining fresh coriander leaves.

CHAPTER 5
Vegetable Sides

Sweet Potato Dauphinois

Serves 4

For a vegetarian version, omit the chorizo sausage and sprinkle grated ginger between the layers of sweet potato.

3 medium (900g) sweet potatoes, peeled and sliced (2mm thin)

1 garlic clove, crushed

100g chorizo sausage, finely sliced

150ml cream

50ml milk

25g butter, cubed

salt and freshly cracked black pepper

Preheat the oven to 180°C/350°F/gas mark 4.

1 Grease a 30cm x 20cm ovenproof dish and cover the base with overlapping slices of potato. Season between layers with salt, pepper and garlic. Cover each layer with a few slices of chorizo.

2 Mix the cream and milk together and pour some over each layer.

3 Repeat the layers with the remaining ingredients and finish with a few slices of chorizo placed on the top.

4 Lightly fleck the surface with butter.

5 Cover with a lid (or parchment paper then foil, which stops the paper flying off in a fan oven).

6 Bake for 1¼ hours. Remove the paper and foil and bake for a further 10 minutes, until just catching colour on top.

Baked Home Fries

Serves 4

For added nutrition, leave the potato skins on.

4 tbsp sunflower oil

2 cloves garlic, peeled and sliced

4 large potatoes, peeled and cut into 2cm cubes

salt and freshly cracked black pepper

Preheat the oven to 220°C/425°F/gas mark 7.

1 Infuse the sunflower oil with the sliced garlic for 10 minutes, then strain (i.e. discard the garlic).

2 Pour the flavoured oil into a deep roasting tray and place in a hot oven for 2 minutes.

3 Remove the tray from the oven, add the cubed potatoes and coat well in the oil. Season with salt and pepper.

4 Return the roasting tray to the oven and roast the potatoes for 15–20 minutes (to ensure the potatoes roast evenly, toss occasionally during cooking).

5 Once crisp and golden, serve immediately.

IF YOU CUT THE POTATOES IN ADVANCE, IMMERSE THEM IN COLD WATER SO THEY DO NOT TURN BROWN (PAT THEM DRY BEFORE USE).

Pea Purée

Serves 4

This is a lovely accompaniment to almost any fish dish. Spoon into metal tian rings (if you have them) and lift off just before serving.

450g frozen garden peas

30g butter, softened

5g mint, leaves chopped

salt and freshly cracked black pepper

1 Boil the frozen peas in boiling water for 5–8 minutes (or according to packet instructions) and drain.

2 Mix in the butter and mint. Purée with a handheld blender and season to taste.

LARGE SCONE CUTTERS OR RAMEKINS CAN BE SUBSTITUTED FOR TIAN RINGS.

Tender Sweet Greens

Serves 4

A classic side dish from our Quick Entertaining courses.

1 tbsp olive oil

20g butter

4 spring onions, sliced diagonally into 3cm lengths

50ml dry white wine

1/2 tsp sugar

200g petit pois (or peas), frozen

200g tender leaf spinach

salt and freshly cracked black
pepper

1 Melt the olive oil and half the butter in a large non-stick pan.

2 Add the spring onions and fry gently for 3–4 minutes. Season with salt and pepper.

3 Turn up the heat, add the wine and sugar, bring to the boil and simmer for 3–4 minutes. Add the frozen peas and spinach and stir until the spinach starts to wilt down and the peas are cooked and a vibrant green in colour.

4 Add a cube of butter (or a drizzle of good-quality olive oil), season and serve.

Potato and Apple Mash

Serves 4

Our Winter Soups and Casseroles course would not be complete without a few nice mash ideas, and this is one of them. A great dish with pork.

700g floury potatoes, peeled and cut into large cubes

200g apples, peeled, cored and sliced

2 tbsp water

150ml milk

50g butter (plus more as required)

salt and freshly cracked black pepper

1 Steam the potatoes for approximately 15 minutes, until soft. Add a small cube of butter, cover and keep warm.

2 Heat the apples in a saucepan with the water. Cover and cook for 5 minutes, until the apples soften and break down. Add to the potatoes.

3 Heat the milk and butter in a saucepan to just below boiling point.

4 Season and mash the potatoes and apple with the hot milk until light and fluffy. Serve in a warm serving bowl. Make a well in the centre and add a small knob of butter to melt into the mash.

IF YOUR STEAMER IS SET OVER A SAUCEPAN, YOU CAN SAVE ON WASHING UP BY PLACING THE COOKED POTATOES AND APPLES INTO ONE SIDE OF THE SAUCEPAN. MOVE THE SAUCEPAN SO THAT ONLY ONE EDGE IS OVER THE HEAT SOURCE AND HEAT THE MILK AND BUTTER BEFORE MASHING EVERYTHING TOGETHER.

Warm Puy Lentils

Serves 4

Warm Puy lentils are a wonderfully healthy and satisfying accompaniment to serve during the winter months.

1 tbsp olive oil

10g butter

1 small leek, finely sliced

1 stalk celery, finely diced

1 carrot, finely diced

2 cloves garlic, chopped

200g Puy lentils

2 bay leaves

2 sprigs fresh thyme

600ml vegetable stock, hot

5 sprigs flat leaf parsley, leaves chopped

salt and freshly cracked black pepper

1 Heat the olive oil and butter in a saucepan and sweat the leek, celery and carrot for 2 minutes. Season, add the garlic and stir for another few minutes.

2 Add the lentils, bay leaves, thyme and the hot stock. Bring to the boil and simmer, uncovered, for 25–30 minutes, until the lentils are al dente (not hard and not mushy) and the liquid has evaporated. Remove the bay leaves and thyme. Just before serving, stir in the chopped parsley.

LENTILS ARE ONE OF THE WORLD'S SUPERFOODS. EXTREMELY GOOD FOR YOU, THEY ARE A SOURCE OF VITAMIN B1, IRON, MAGNESIUM AND DIETARY FIBRE.

Mangetout with Ginger and Orange

Serves 4

This is a handy number to make use of the microwave when you want to save space in the oven to heat plates.

½ unwaxed orange

150g mangetout

1 tsp freshly grated root ginger (or to taste)

10g butter

salt and freshly cracked black pepper

1 Finely zest the orange, then squeeze the juice from it.
2 Place the zest, orange juice, mangetout, ginger and butter in a bowl and season. Cover with cling film and set aside until ready to use.
3 When ready to serve, heat in the microwave on full power for 90 seconds, or longer, until the mangetout are cooked.

UNWAXED ORANGES AND LEMONS AREN'T SPRAYED WITH AS MANY PESTICIDES AS THE WAXED ONES. IF YOU ARE USING THE ZEST IN A RECIPE AND CAN ONLY GET THE WAXED VARIETY, POUR BOILING WATER OVER THEM TO SOFTEN THE WAX AND RUB THE SKIN WITH A DRY CLOTH.

Roast Tomatoes

Serves 4

These tomatoes can be served either warm or cold and are a great accompaniment to almost any meat or fish dish.

300g vine tomatoes

2 garlic cloves, thinly sliced

1 sprig fresh thyme (or oregano),
   leaves only

4 tbsp extra virgin olive oil

sea salt and freshly cracked
   black pepper

Preheat the oven to 140°C/275°F/gas mark 1.

1 Halve the tomatoes lengthways, cutting out the stalk ends in neat V shapes.

2 Arrange the tomatoes cut side up on a baking sheet lined with parchment paper.

3 Scatter slices of garlic over each tomato, along with some thyme leaves.

4 Drizzle with olive oil and season.

5 Roast in the oven for 30–35 minutes – the tomatoes should still retain their shape.

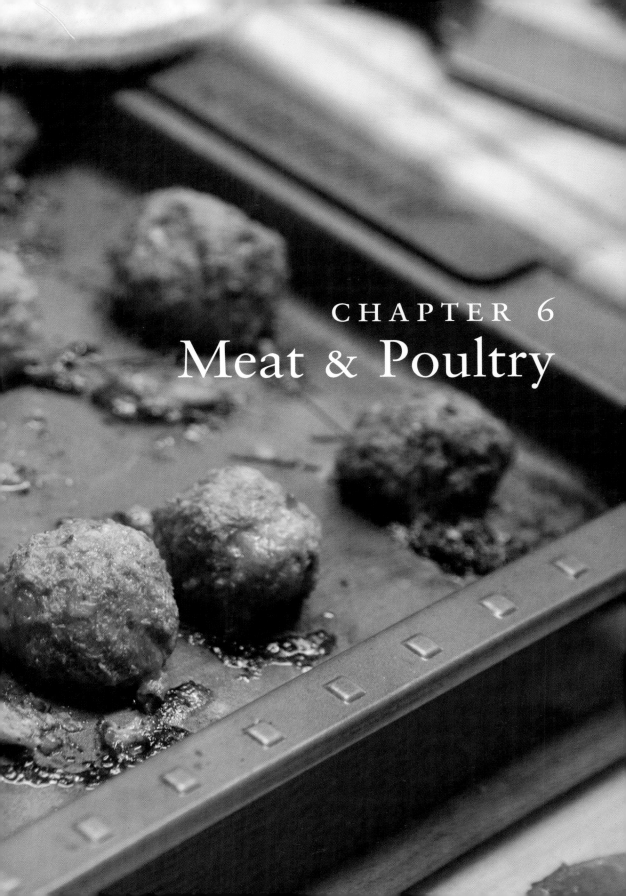

CHAPTER 6
Meat & Poultry

Lamb Pie

Serves 4

For larger numbers, take the convenient option and prop individual puff pastry lids over this hearty filling as a substitute for the shortcrust pastry. To do this, use ready rolled puff pastry, cut out triangles, brush with egg and bake in the oven until puffed up and golden.

10g butter

1 tbsp sunflower oil

450g diced lamb, coated in seasoned flour

250ml red wine

500ml chicken stock, hot

100g baby turnips, peeled and cut into 2cm cubes

1 carrot, peeled and cut into chunks (or 6 baby carrots, halved)

2 stalks celery, roughly chopped

200g baby onions, peeled and left whole

10g fresh oregano (or thyme), leaves only

200g shortcrust pastry (see p.190) rolled out to 2mm thick

1 egg, lightly whisked with milk, to wash over the pastry

salt and freshly cracked black pepper

Preheat the oven to 180°C/350°F/gas mark 4.

1 Heat the butter and oil in a large heavy-based casserole. Over a high heat, add the lamb in 2 batches and brown quickly on all sides (to avoid the meat cooking through). Transfer the browned meat onto a plate between batches.

2 Return the lamb to the pot and add the wine and hot stock. Cover, bring to the boil and simmer for 15 minutes.

3 Add the turnip, carrot, celery and onions and season with salt and pepper. Cover and simmer for 5 minutes.

4 Using a slotted spoon, transfer the meat and vegetables to an ovenproof dish (or individual pie dishes). Continue simmering the liquid, uncovered, until it has reduced and thickened before pouring it and the oregano (or thyme) over the pie filling (avoid totally submerging the filling).

5 Lay the pastry over the filling and cut to fit the outline of the dish, making 2 slits in the centre (to allow steam to escape). Trim away any overhanging pastry using the back of a sharp knife. Crimp the edges with the back of a fork and glaze the surface of the pastry with egg wash.

6 Bake in the oven for 45 minutes, or until the pastry is golden.

WHEN SEALING THE MEAT, AVOID OVERCROWDING THE POT OR THE MEAT WILL STEAM RATHER THAN BROWN.

Lasagne al Forno

Serves 4

Our students love this classic yet simple lasagne. The sauce is quick and easy, as there is very little chopping of vegetables. I tend to make it in larger quantities and freeze it in batches for making spaghetti alla Bolognese.

2 tbsp olive oil

1 onion, chopped

450g round steak, minced

2–3 tbsp tomato purée

1 x 400g tin chopped tomatoes

400ml water

1 bay leaf

250g lasagne sheets

150g red cheddar cheese or Parmesan, grated

WHITE SAUCE

75g butter, cut into pieces

75g plain flour

1.2 litres milk

salt and freshly cracked black pepper

....

A RAGÚ SAUCE IS THE TRUE NAME FOR THE MEAT-BASED BOLOGNESE SAUCE. YOU CAN ADD GARLIC, CHOPPED CARROTS, SLICED MUSHROOMS, HERBS SUCH AS OREGANO OR EVEN RED WINE – WHATEVER MAKES IT YOUR IDEAL RAGÚ SAUCE.

Preheat the oven to 190°C/375°F/gas mark 5.

1 To prepare the sauce, melt the butter in a saucepan. Stir in the flour and cook for 1–2 minutes, stirring constantly. Over a medium-high heat, gradually add the milk, stirring constantly. When all the milk is incorporated, lower the heat, add the seasoning and simmer gently until the sauce thickens. Remove from the heat and allow to cool slightly. (For a quicker method, make the white sauce by putting the butter, flour and milk (cold) in a medium pan and cook over a medium heat, whisking until thickened and smooth. Remove from the heat and season.)

2 Heat 1 tbsp of oil in a heavy-based saucepan and gently fry the onion for 5 minutes, until translucent. Increase the heat, stir in the minced beef and cook until brown and crumbled. Season well.

3 Stir in the tomato purée to coat the meat (the paste should give the meat a red hue), then add the tomatoes, water (much of this will evaporate during the long simmer) and bay leaf. Bring to the boil, then fast simmer, uncovered, for at least 45 minutes. Remove the bay leaf.

4 Spoon the meat sauce over the base of an ovenproof dish. Cover with non-overlapping sheets of lasagne.

5 Add a third of each ingredient in layers (adding layers of ragú sauce, white sauce, cheese and lasagne sheets, in that order), seasoning well between layers. Finish with a layer of lasagne covered in white sauce and a sprinkling of cheese (avoid overfilling the dish to prevent leakage).

6 Loosely cover with tin foil and bake for 45 minutes. Remove the tin foil for the last 15 minutes for a golden crust. Allow to sit for 15 minutes before serving.

Tex-Mex Chilli with Jacket Potatoes

Serves 4

Once you get known for this Tex-Mex chilli con carne, you can serve it in flour tortillas or tacos with grated cheese and avocado salsa (see p. 131). This recipe makes quite a lot, but it's definitely worth freezing any leftovers.

2 tbsp olive oil

1 large onion, chopped

600g round steak, minced

2 cloves garlic, crushed

1 tsp ground cumin

1 green pepper, deseeded and sliced

2 red chillies, chopped (seeds left in)

2 tbsp tomato purée

1 x 400g tin chopped tomatoes

1 x 330ml tin ale (e.g. Smithwicks) or beer/lager

1 x 400g tin red kidney beans, drained

1 tsp brown sugar (optional)

4 large baking potatoes, skins scrubbed clean

100ml crème fraîche, to serve

50g mature red cheddar cheese, coarsely grated

1 tbsp freshly chopped herbs (coriander or parsley or chives)

salt and freshly cracked black pepper

Preheat the oven to 200°C/400°F/gas mark 6.

1 Heat the oil in a large saucepan and gently fry the onion for 5 minutes, until translucent, before adding in the minced beef and garlic. Stir well, breaking up the meat, until brown and crumbled.

2 Stir in the cumin, green pepper, red chillies, tomato purée, chopped tomatoes and ale. Cover and bring to the boil before simmering for 30 minutes.

3 Add the kidney beans and simmer uncovered for a further 10 minutes and season to taste (add the brown sugar if required).

4 Pierce each potato deeply with a skewer or fork and bake at 200°C/400°F/gas mark 6, for 1–1½ hours (depending on their size), until the skin is crisp and a skewer slides in easily. Turn down the oven and keep the potatoes warm.

5 Cut a cross in each baked potato and prise it open slightly. Spoon the chilli over the potato with a spoonful of crème fraîche, some grated cheese and fresh herbs.

Beef Stroganoff

Serves 4

This much-loved classic is perfect for serving at a buffet. While easily scaled up to feed larger groups, be careful when doubling up on the stock and cream, as you won't need as much.

600g beef (round steak), sliced into 4mm-wide strips, or cubed

2 tbsp seasoned flour

3 tbsp sunflower oil (plus more if required for browning meat)

50g butter

150g shallots, peeled and very thinly sliced

2 tbsp paprika

250g mushrooms, wiped clean and sliced thinly

200ml beef stock

8–10 drops Tabasco sauce

2 tsp lemon juice

200ml sour cream (or crème fraîche or double cream)

10g flat leaf parsley, leaves chopped

salt and freshly cracked black pepper

Preheat the oven to 180°C/350°F/gas mark 4.

1 Coat the meat in seasoned flour.

2 Over a high heat, add 1 tbsp of oil to a heavy-based frying pan and fry the meat briskly in 3–4 batches, until the meat is just sealed on the outside. Transfer the meat to a plate after each batch.

3 Wipe the pan clean. Heat the butter and gently fry the shallots for 10 minutes, stirring in the paprika towards the end. Set aside. Increase the heat and add the mushrooms and sauté briskly for a few minutes, until the mushrooms develop a golden colour.

4 In a casserole, combine the shallots, mushrooms and beef. Add the stock and Tabasco, bring to the boil and simmer for 2 minutes, until slightly thickened. Taste for seasoning, adding the lemon juice and a little more Tabasco if required.

5 Transfer the casserole to a preheated oven and cook for 1 hour (or slightly longer if the pieces of meat are large). Remove from the oven and stir in the sour cream and chopped parsley. Serve with rice and roast tomatoes (see p. 92).

TRADITIONALLY A RUSSIAN DISH MADE WITH FILLET STEAK, THIS RECIPE IS SLOW COOKED WITH MORE ECONOMICAL ROUND STEAK. PLACING THE MEAT AND FLOUR IN A PLASTIC BAG AND GIVING IT A GOOD SHAKE WILL COAT THE MEAT EVENLY.

Chicken and Shellfish Paella

Serves 4

If you can't get fresh mussels, you can substitute clams.

12 fresh mussels

8–12 uncooked tiger prawns (if frozen, thoroughly defrosted)

pinch saffron strands (approximately 10–15 strands)

200ml white wine

500ml chicken stock (plus a little more if required), hot

3 skinless chicken breasts, cut into thick strips

3 tbsp olive oil

1 onion, diced

1 red pepper, finely sliced lengthways

100g chorizo sausage, peeled and sliced thinly

250g basmati rice

4 garlic cloves, crushed

1/2 tsp chilli flakes

1 tbsp fresh oregano leaves

4 tomatoes, quartered

80g frozen peas, defrosted

2 lemons, cut into wedges

5 sprigs flat leaf parsley, leaves chopped

salt and freshly cracked black pepper

1 Scrub and debeard the mussels.

2 Remove the heads from the prawns and release them from their shells. Devein them by making a slit along their backs using a small, sharp knife and remove any dark thread (the intestine) with the knife tip. Refrigerate all the shellfish.

3 Add the saffron and wine to the hot stock and allow to infuse. Meanwhile, season the chicken strips with pepper and heat 2 tbsp of olive oil in a paella pan (or a large non-stick pan) over a high heat and seal the outside of the chicken strips, until golden, and set aside on a plate.

4 With the remaining olive oil, fry the onions with the red pepper and chorizo for 10 minutes, until softened. Stir in the rice, garlic, chilli, oregano, tomatoes and infused hot stock. Cover and simmer over a medium-high heat for 15–20 minutes, until the rice is cooked, adding some boiling water if the paella starts to dry out while simmering.

5 Scatter in the chicken and mussels. Cover and simmer for 10 minutes, until the meat is cooked and most of the mussel shells have opened (discard any mussels that haven't opened). Lastly, add the prawns and peas and cook for a further 2–3 minutes, until the prawns turn pink. Check the seasoning and serve immediately, garnished with wedges of lemon and freshly chopped parsley.

BUTTERFLYING THE PRAWNS GIVES AN ATTRACTIVE FINISH TO THE PAELLA, WHERE THE PRAWNS FAN OUT AND TURN PINK WHEN COOKED.

Chicken Breasts Wrapped in Parma Ham

Serves 4

4 large chicken breasts

125g goat's cheese, rind removed

8–10 semi-sun-dried (sunblush) tomatoes, patted dry

3 sprigs fresh basil, leaves only

8 slices Parma ham

extra virgin olive oil, as required

salt and freshly cracked black pepper

FOR THE COUSCOUS

225g (8oz) couscous

400ml vegetable stock, hot

1 tsp freshly chopped chives

Preheat the oven to 180°C/350°F/gas mark 4.

1 Using a sharp knife, cut deeply horizontally through the side of each chicken breast to form a deep pocket. Stuff with a spoonful of goat's cheese, 2 semi-sun-dried tomatoes and a few basil leaves. Season and seal the pocket to cover the filling. Place each chicken breast on 2 overlapping pieces of Parma ham and wrap up. Place presentation side up on a baking sheet and bake in the oven for 30 minutes, until the chicken is cooked through.

2 While the chicken is in the oven, place the couscous in a heatproof bowl and cover with boiling stock. Cover the bowl tightly with cling film and leave to stand for 10 minutes, until all the water is absorbed, then fluff it up with a fork and sprinkle with the chives.

3 Slice each chicken breast at an angle and arrange on a bed of couscous. Drizzle with some extra virgin olive oil and garnish with basil leaves.

Chicken with Cashew Nuts

Serves 4

1 tbsp cornflour

2 egg whites

4 chicken breasts, trimmed and cut across the grain into 3mm-thin strips

4 tbsp groundnut oil

120g unroasted cashew nuts

2 cloves garlic, crushed

1 red chilli, deseeded and finely chopped

8 spring onions, cut diagonally into 2cm lengths

1 level tbsp cornflour blended with 1 tbsp water

SAUCE

500ml chicken stock

90ml (6 tbsp) lemon juice

3 tbsp brown sugar

3 tbsp light soy sauce

3 tbsp saké (or dry sherry)

1 In a bowl, stir the cornflour into the egg whites until dissolved. Add the chicken and stir until well coated.

2 Combine all the sauce ingredients.

3 In a wok or large non-stick pan, heat the oil until it is quite hot (but not smoking). Stir-fry the cashew nuts until golden in colour. Add the garlic and chilli and stir-fry for 1 minute longer.

4 Next, add the chicken and stir continuously until the chicken turns an opaque colour (this takes about 3–4 minutes, depending on how crowded the pan is).

5 Next, add the spring onions and the sauce and bring to the boil over a high heat before adding the cornflour and water mixture. Simmer for 3 minutes, until the sauce thickens slightly. Serve immediately with rice and steamed pak choi.

LIGHT SOY SAUCE IS OFTEN USED INSTEAD OF DARK SOY SAUCE WHEN YOU WANT THE FINISHED DISH TO HAVE A LIGHTER COLOUR.

Turkey Fricassée

Serves 4

If you have leftover turkey after Christmas Day, this is an ideal way to use it up. Delicious comfort food.

600g cooked turkey meat (or use uncooked turkey breasts), torn into pieces

3–4 tbsp olive oil

250g button mushrooms, halved

3 smoked rashers, cut into small squares

1 medium onion, sliced

200ml dry white wine

250ml chicken stock

salt and freshly cracked black pepper

WHITE SAUCE

25g butter

1 tbsp flour

400ml milk

1 If you are using uncooked turkey breasts, trim them of any sinew, drizzle with olive oil and season with salt and pepper. Cook in the oven at 180°C/350°F/gas mark 4 for 10 minutes, then continue as per the recipe with cooked turkey.

2 To make the white sauce, melt the butter in a small saucepan. Stir in the flour and cook for 1–2 minutes. Over a medium-high heat, gradually add all the milk, stirring vigorously to avoid any lumps forming. When the mixture thickens and bubbles, remove from the heat.

3 In a large saucepan over a high heat, add half the oil and sauté the mushrooms and rashers for 5 minutes. Season well, transfer to a plate and set aside.

4 Heat the remaining oil in the saucepan and lightly sauté the onion for 5 minutes, without browning. Add the wine and simmer over a medium high heat for 10 minutes.

5 Stir in the turkey, mushrooms, rashers, chicken stock and white sauce. Cover and bring the fricassée to the boil. Turn down the heat and simmer gently for approximately 20–25 minutes, stirring regularly. Check the seasoning and serve with long grain rice or even baked potatoes (see p. 99) and some green beans.

Beef Casserole with Horseradish Crème Fraîche

Serves 4

If cooking for children, feel free to reduce the amount of wine and increase the amount of stock. If you choose to omit the potatoes from inside the casserole, serve with some mashed potato flavoured with the horseradish sauce.

3 tbsp sunflower oil (or olive oil)

750g stewing beef, cut into bite-sized cubes

4 stalks celery, cut into chunks

1 large onion, sliced

3 cloves garlic, chopped

2 sprigs fresh thyme

1 bay leaf

1 heaped tbsp flour

300ml beef stock, hot

300ml red wine

2 tsp tomato purée

4–6 baby carrots, peeled and left whole

250g baby potatoes, halved lengthways

5 sprigs flat leaf parsley, leaves chopped

salt and freshly cracked black pepper

HORSERADISH SAUCE

1 tbsp horseradish sauce

2 tbsp crème fraîche

Preheat the oven to 160°C/325°F/gas mark 3.

1 Heat 2 tbsp of the oil in a large, heavy-bottomed casserole. Over a high heat, add the cubes of meat in batches and brown quickly on all sides (to avoid the meat cooking through). Transfer the browned meat onto a plate between batches.

2 Deglaze the pan with a splash of wine or stock. Reduce the heat, add the remaining oil to the casserole and sauté the celery, onion, garlic, thyme and bay leaf, stirring well for 5 minutes, until starting to brown.

3 Return the meat along with any juices to the casserole. Add the flour and stir for 2 minutes (this gets rid of the raw flour taste).

4 Add the hot stock, wine and tomato purée and season well.

5 Cover and bring to the boil before transferring to the oven to cook for 2 hours (alternatively, leave on a low simmer on the hob for the same length of time). Stir occasionally and add the carrots and potatoes for the last 40 minutes of cooking.

6 To make the horseradish sauce, mix together the horseradish sauce and crème fraîche. Refrigerate.

7 To serve, remove the sprig of thyme and bay leaf from the casserole, garnish with fresh parsley and serve with a spoonful of horseradish sauce.

DEGLAZING IS A THRIFTY AND SIMPLE PROCESS OF ADDING WINE OR STOCK TO THE PAN AFTER BROWNING MEAT. SCRAPING OFF THE CARAMELISED MEAT JUICES LEFT IN THE PAN ENSURES THE CONCENTRATED FLAVOURS ARE CONSERVED.

Sesame Pork Stir-Fry

Serves 4

Sesame seeds are high in polyunsaturated fatty acids. Sprinkling them over stir-fries couldn't be easier.

100ml soy sauce

2 tbsp toasted sesame oil

5cm piece fresh root ginger, peeled and thinly sliced

2 cloves garlic, chopped

500g pork tenderloin fillet, trimmed of fat

2 tbsp sesame seeds

1 carrot, cut into batons (thick matchsticks)

75g mangetout

75g baby corn, sliced in half lengthways

3 spring onions, sliced into 3cm diagonals

100g broccoli, cut into florets and florets sliced in half

1 Mix together the soy sauce, sesame oil, ginger and garlic in a shallow bowl.

2 Slice the pork crossways into thin slices and add to the marinade. Season with black pepper and set aside for 10 minutes.

3 Heat a wok or large non-stick frying pan over a medium heat. Add the sesame seeds (there's no need for oil) and stir for 2 minutes, or until evenly toasted. Transfer to a plate.

4 Using a slotted spoon, remove the pork from the marinade and in a hot frying pan, seal the pork in batches until browned all over. Remove and set aside along with any juices from the pan.

5 Add all the vegetables to the hot pan, pour over the remaining marinade and stir-fry for a few minutes. Toss in the pork and stir-fry for a few minutes more, until the pork is just cooked through.

6 Serve immediately with a sprinkling of toasted sesame seeds and some noodles.

ROASTING TINY SESAME SEEDS WITHOUT BURNING THEM REQUIRES CARE, BUT ONCE ROASTED, THEIR NUTTY AROMA IS MAGICALLY UNLOCKED.

Lamb Kofta

Serves 4 (makes 20 balls)

Ideal as a starter, these kofta can also be served as party finger food with a mint raita dip.

1 tbsp olive oil

1 onion, very finely chopped

3 cloves garlic, chopped

5cm piece ginger, freshly grated

1 chilli, finely chopped

3 tsp ground cumin

1 tsp ground coriander

500g minced lamb

80g breadcrumbs

15g mint, leaves chopped

1 egg, lightly whisked

salt and freshly cracked black
  pepper

Preheat the oven to 200°C/400°F/gas mark 6.

1 Heat the olive oil in a non-stick frying pan and gently sweat the onion, garlic and ginger for 10 minutes, until softened. Add the chilli, cumin and ground coriander and stir-fry for 1 minute. Transfer to a large bowl.

2 Add all the remaining ingredients (adding the egg last to bind the mixture), seasoning well with salt and pepper. Roll into 15–20 balls and place on a baking tray in the oven for 20 minutes, or until cooked through (alternatively, fry in batches until cooked through and nicely browned).

3 Serve with mint raita (p.198).

Pasta with Chorizo and Rocket

Serves 4

For a party, this recipe can be easily adapted to serve more people. In this case, multiply the recipe upwards for the number of guests and include some chopped celery and chicken strips to the frying pan. Stir through a generous amount of reduced cream at the end.

100g chorizo sausage, peeled and diced

2 tbsp olive oil

1 red onion, halved and thinly sliced

2 cloves of garlic, crushed

3 tbsp semi-sun-dried (sunblush) tomatoes

300ml white wine

300g pasta (linguine is our choice for this dish)

50g fresh rocket leaves

75g Parmesan shavings

salt and freshly cracked black pepper

1 Dry fry the chorizo in a heavy-based frying pan for 5 minutes, until just becoming crisp (do not allow to burn). Remove to a sheet of absorbent kitchen paper with a slotted spoon and keep warm.

2 Gently fry the onion in the olive oil for 10 minutes, adding in the garlic towards the end.

3 Drain and roughly chop the semi-sun-dried tomatoes before adding them to the onion along with the wine and season with salt and pepper. Increase the heat and simmer for a few minutes. Remove from the heat.

4 Bring a large pot of salted water to the boil. Add the pasta and simmer for 10–12 minutes, until al dente (or cook as per packet instructions). Once cooked, drain the pasta and while still hot, return it to the saucepan over a medium heat. Drizzle with a slick of olive oil.

5 Stir in the sauce mixture, the crispy chorizo and lastly the rocket (if the rocket leaves are very large, roughly chop them). Serve in pasta bowls, season with cracked black pepper and garnish with Parmesan shavings.

THE BEST-QUALITY PARMESAN IS KNOWN AS PARMIGIANO REGGIANO. HOWEVER, GRANA PADANO IS ANOTHER HARD-GRATING CHEESE THAT'S USUALLY CHEAPER AND IN MANY CASES WILL SUBSTITUTE JUST AS WELL.

Spaghetti Carbonara

Serves 4

The true Italian version of carbonara uses no cream! Other types of pasta, such as linguine, tagliatelle or even fettuccine, would work equally well.

300g pasta (spaghetti)

2 tbsp olive oil mixed with a small knob of butter

8 hickory smoked rashers, cut into small cubes (or lardons fumé or smoked pancetta)

1 tsp dried chilli flakes

2 cloves garlic, crushed

4 eggs, lightly whisked

100g Parmesan, very finely grated

salt and freshly cracked black pepper

1 Bring a large pot of water to the boil, add a dessertspoon of salt and return to a simmer before adding the pasta and cooking for 10–12 minutes, until al dente (or cook as per packet instructions).

2 While the pasta is cooking, whisk the eggs, finely grate the Parmesan, crush the garlic and cut up the rashers.

3 Over a medium heat, fry the rashers and chillies in the olive oil for 8 minutes, adding the garlic towards the end. Remove from the heat, set aside and keep warm.

4 Once cooked, drain the pasta and while still hot, return it to the saucepan over a medium heat. Drizzle with a slick of olive oil and immediately add the eggs and quickly stir through the pasta for 1 minute. As soon as the eggs start to turn opaque, turn off the heat and stir in the Parmesan until it melts. Lastly, stir in the fried ingredients. Season and serve immediately.

THE CREAMINESS IN THIS CARBONARA IS DUE TO THE EGGS NOT BEING OVERCOOKED. REMOVE THE SAUCEPAN FROM THE HEAT JUST BEFORE YOU SEE THE EGG STARTING TO SCRAMBLE.

Pasta all'Amatriciana

Serves 4

This is another store cupboard favourite for a family meal. Smoked rashers can be used if you don't have any pancetta. However, it's a good idea to buy sliced pancetta and keep it in the freezer.

1 tbsp olive oil

100g smoked pancetta, diced

1 onion, finely diced

3 cloves garlic, crushed

1 tsp chilli flakes (or to taste)

1 x 400g tin chopped tomatoes

100ml red wine

1/2 tsp sugar (add only if required)

300g pasta (pappardelle, spaghetti or linguine)

100g pecorino Romano cheese (or Parmesan), freshly grated

salt and freshly cracked black pepper

1 Over a medium-high heat, cook the diced pancetta in olive oil for 5 minutes. Remove to a sheet of absorbent kitchen paper with a slotted spoon and keep warm.

2 Fry the onion in the same pan, and when it begins to colour (but not burn), add the garlic and chilli flakes. Stir for another 2 minutes before adding the tinned tomatoes, red wine and sugar (if required).

3 Simmer uncovered for 20 minutes, until the liquid has reduced and thickened. Season to taste.

4 Return the pancetta to the pot and heat through.

5 Bring a large pot of salted water to the boil. Add the pasta and simmer for 10–12 minutes, until al dente (or cook as per packet instructions).

6 Once cooked, drain the pasta and while still hot, return it to the saucepan over a medium heat. Drizzle with a slick of olive oil and add the sauce. Stir until the pasta is fully coated, and serve with the grated pecorino.

PECORINO ROMANO IS A HARD GRATING CHEESE MADE FROM SHEEP'S MILK. IT CAN OFTEN BE SUBSTITUTED FOR PARMESAN, BUT IT HAS A MUCH SALTIER FLAVOUR.

Duck Breasts with Red Wine Sauce

Serves 4

Starting with an unheated pan is a clean and safe method of achieving a crisp skin with no spitting fat.

10g butter

1 tbsp olive oil

300g small shallots, skinned

$^1/_2$ tsp caster sugar

4 x 230g duck breasts

salt and freshly cracked black pepper

RED WINE SAUCE

150ml red wine

200ml veal stock (or chicken)

1 sprig fresh thyme

15g butter

Preheat the oven to 180°C/350°F/gas mark 4.

1 Melt half the butter with a dash of olive oil in a heavy-based frying pan. Over a medium-high heat, sauté the whole shallots for 5 minutes, turning occasionally. Add the sugar and continue frying until golden brown on the outside. Transfer to a roasting tray and cook the shallots in the oven for 10 minutes, until softened. Keep warm.

2 To make the sauce, heat the red wine in a saucepan and boil vigorously for 10 minutes before adding the stock and thyme. Continue boiling for another 5 minutes, until reduced and syrupy. Remove from the heat, discard the sprig of thyme and add the butter to give a glossy finish to the sauce. Keep warm.

3 Trim each duck breast and with a very sharp knife score the skin in a criss-cross pattern (take care not to pierce through to the flesh). Just before cooking, season the skin of each duck breast and place skin side down in an unheated heavy-based frying pan (or chargrill pan).

4 Heat the pan and allow the fat to render down (pour off the excess rendered fat, which will keep refrigerated for 1–2 weeks and can be used for roast potatoes). Turn each breast over and continue to cook on a medium-heat for 4–5 minutes. Remove from the pan and rest for 10 minutes, loosely tented in kitchen foil. Carve each breast into thin slices and serve with the red wine sauce, shallots, tender sweet greens (see p. 88) and baked home fries (see p. 87).

Chicken and Cannellini Bean Casserole

Serves 4

2 tbsp olive oil

1 onion, diced

4 chicken breasts, cut into strips

2 red peppers, deseeded and cut into thin strips

6 celery stalks, diced

2 garlic cloves, crushed

pinch crushed chilli flakes

450ml chicken stock, hot

1 x 400g tin cannellini beans, drained

1 large sprig fresh sage, leaves roughly chopped

2 tbsp crème fraîche

10g flat leaf parsley, leaves only, roughly chopped

salt and freshly cracked black pepper

1 Heat half the olive oil in a heavy-based saucepan and lightly sauté the onion for 5 minutes.

2 Heat the rest of the oil and fry the chicken for 5 minutes, until the strips are cooked on the outside (turn opaque).

3 Add the peppers, celery, garlic and crushed chilli flakes. Season and continue frying for a further 5 minutes.

4 Add the hot chicken stock, cover and bring to the boil. Pour in the cannellini beans and simmer for 15 minutes before stirring through the sage and crème fraîche.

5 Just before serving, add the chopped parsley. Serve with steamed potatoes and roast tomatoes (see p. 92).

Home-Style Ham with a Honey Glaze

Serves 4

Glazed ham doesn't have to be left until Christmas to be enjoyed. Serve with cabbage, parsley sauce and mashed potato.

1.5kg ham fillet (boneless joint of cured pork leg)

500ml cider (or 1 litre apple juice)

1 onion, quartered

1 stalk celery, halved

1 carrot, halved

1 bay leaf

1 tbsp whole peppercorns

HONEY GLAZE

2 tbsp honey

2 tsp English mustard

10 cloves

1 To reduce the saltiness of the ham, soak it in cold water in the fridge for at least 6 hours, preferably overnight. Throw away the soaking water.

2 To cook the ham, place the fillet skin side up in a large, deep saucepan. Add the cider, onion, celery, carrot, bay leaf and peppercorns and enough cold water to just cover the ham.

3 Cover with a lid and bring to the boil before reducing the heat to a simmer for 45 minutes per kilo (or 20 minutes per lb) plus an extra 20 minutes of simmering at the end.

4 Remove the ham from the water and allow to stand for 10 minutes before carving (unless glazing first).

5 To glaze, allow the ham to cool completely and peel the tough outer skin away with a sharp knife, leaving a thick layer of fat. Lightly score the fat in a criss-cross pattern at 2cm intervals. Smear honey and mustard generously over the surface. Randomly stick cloves into the surface.

6 Place the ham under a hot grill until the top is caramelised, basting from time to time with the deliciously sweet juices collecting around the ham (for a large ham, use the grill setting inside the main oven if this is available).

Method to bake in the oven: Wrap in tin foil, put on a roasting tray and bake at 180°C/350°F/gas mark 4 for 55 minutes per kg, plus 25 minutes. Leave to rest for 15–30 minutes before carving.

IF SHORT OF TIME OR SPACE IN YOUR FRIDGE, PLACE THE HAM IN A POT OF WATER, COVER AND BRING TO THE BOIL, THEN DRAIN OFF THE SOAKING WATER BEFORE COOKING THE HAM IN STEP 2.

Catalina Chicken

Serves 4

My grandmother's recipe. She always serves this to us with homemade chips, which she cuts by hand with a crinkle cutter.

25g butter

1 tbsp olive oil

200g mushrooms, quartered

1 onion, diced

1 tbsp plain flour

500ml dry cider

200ml chicken stock

1 tbsp tomato purée

1 tsp sugar

1 tsp white wine vinegar

1 tsp paprika

1/2 tsp chilli powder

4 free-range chicken breasts, part boned, skin removed

1 red pepper, deseeded and cut into chunks

3 sprigs flat leaf parsley, leaves chopped

salt and freshly cracked black pepper

Preheat the oven to 170°C/325°F/gas mark 3.

1 In a heavy-based frying pan, heat the butter with a dash of olive oil and sauté the mushrooms over a high heat until they turn golden on the outside. Set aside.

2 Lower the heat, add a little more olive oil and sweat the onions for 5 minutes before stirring in the flour and cooking for 2 minutes more.

3 Increase the heat, add the cider and stock and simmer for 10 minutes to reduce the liquid slightly.

4 Meanwhile, mix together the tomato purée, sugar, vinegar, paprika and chilli powder and stir through the cider sauce. Season to taste.

5 Remove the skin from the chicken breasts and season them. Arrange the chicken in a single layer in an ovenproof dish. Scatter over the peppers and mushrooms and cover with the sauce.

6 Cover and cook in the oven for 1 hour, stirring halfway through. Just before serving, stir in the chopped parsley.

7 Serve with baked home fries (see p. 87) or baked potatoes (see p. 99).

Moussaka

Serves 4

I have often enjoyed moussaka on the Greek Islands, where they include a layer of potatoes in their version.

2 medium aubergines, stalk and base removed

2 tbsp olive oil (for brushing aubergines and frying onion)

1 onion, chopped

1 garlic clove, crushed

500g lamb mince (or beef mince)

1 tsp ground allspice (or ground cinnamon)

3 sprigs flat leaf parsley, leaves chopped

2 tbsp tomato purée

1 x 400g tin chopped tomatoes

salt and freshly cracked black pepper

WHITE SAUCE

75g butter

75g flour

1.2 litres milk

1 egg yolk

Preheat the oven to 180°C/350°F/gas mark 4.

1 Slice the aubergines into 1cm thick rounds, brush both sides with olive oil and place on a baking sheet. Season well and roast in the oven for 20 minutes, until golden.

2 Heat 1 tbsp of oil in a heavy-based saucepan and gently sweat the onion for 10 minutes, adding the garlic towards the end. Increase the heat and stir in the minced meat and cook until brown and crumbled. Add the allspice, parsley, tomato purée and chopped tomatoes. Simmer for 10 minutes and season well.

3 In an ovenproof dish, add alternate layers of meat and aubergines (overlap if necessary), starting and ending with a layer of meat.

4 To prepare the white sauce, melt the butter in a saucepan. Stir in the flour and cook for 1–2 minutes, stirring constantly. Over a medium-high heat, gradually add the milk, stirring constantly. When all the milk is incorporated, lower the heat, add the seasoning and simmer gently, until the sauce thickens. Remove from the heat and allow to cool slightly. (For a quicker method, make white sauce by putting the milk (cold), butter and flour in a medium pan and cook over a medium heat, whisking until thickened and smooth. Remove from the heat and season.)

5 Beat the egg yolk in a bowl, then beat a few spoons of the sauce into the egg. Stir this mixture back into the sauce.

6 Spoon the sauce over the layered filling and bake in the oven for 30 minutes (the topping will have risen and become golden). Remove from the oven and leave to rest for 5 minutes before serving.

Steak with Pepper Sauce

Serves 4

This is one of my family favourites. A hearty, rich dish and a perfect Friday reward for a hard week's work. Serve with tender sweet greens (see p.88) and baked home fries (see p.87).

2 tbsp whole black peppercorns

sea salt

1 tbsp olive oil

4 x 200g sirloin steaks

SAUCE

200ml white wine

250ml chicken stock

200ml double cream

1 Place the peppercorns between 2 sheets of cling film and bash with a rolling pin (until only half the peppercorns remain whole). Place the peppercorns on a plate and lightly coat each steak on both sides with them. Lightly season with sea salt.

2 Heat the oil in a large heavy-based frying pan over a high heat. Fry the steaks for 3 minutes on each side, then remove from the pan and set aside on a plate.

3 Deglaze the pan with wine, then add the chicken stock, cream and any peppercorns from the plate and simmer for 5–10 minutes, until the sauce has reduced and thickened.

4 Return the steak to the pan of cream sauce. Continue cooking the steaks according to each person's taste (rare, medium, well done) while spooning the sauce over the steaks to coat well (if the steak has too many peppercorns on it, scrape them back into the sauce).

5 Serve immediately on hot plates drizzled with the peppercorn sauce.

HAVE A PEPPER MILL HANDY TO COARSELY GRIND SOME EXTRA PEPPER OVER THE STEAKS (IF THE ROLLING PIN IS TOO NOISY!)

CHAPTER 7 Seafood

Prawn Fried Rice

Serves 4

This is a meal in itself. It's important that the rice isn't added hot, or the dish will go mushy. The second secret to success is to have all your ingredients ready before you start stir-frying.

2 tbsp groundnut oil

2 eggs, lightly whisked

1cm piece fresh root ginger, peeled and finely chopped

2 cloves garlic, crushed

350g cooked long grain rice, cold

$\frac{1}{2}$ tsp ground turmeric

6 spring onions, finely chopped

120g frozen peas (preferably petit pois), defrosted

200g cooked prawns

SAUCE

50ml chicken/vegetable stock

50ml rice wine or saké (or use dry sherry)

2 tbsp soy sauce

1 Heat all the sauce ingredients and keep hot.

2 Whisk the eggs and chop the onions.

3 Heat half the groundnut oil in a wok or other large non-stick pan on a high heat (do not allow the oil to smoke). Add the eggs, rocking the pan so the eggs coat it in a thin and even layer before using a wooden spoon to stir-fry and in turn break up the eggs until they are just starting to scramble. Transfer to a plate.

4 Heat the remaining oil in the pan and fry the ginger and garlic before adding the cold rice, turmeric, spring onions and peas. Stir-fry these ingredients over a high heat.

5 Lastly, add the hot sauce, eggs and prawns and heat through. Taste and adjust the seasoning. Serve immediately.

USE A TEASPOON TO PEEL GINGER BY SCRAPING AWAY THE SKIN WITH THE TIP OF THE SPOON.

Madras Fish Curry with Pollack

Serves 4

An ideal quick midweek supper and the fish is easily substituted with chicken.

450g pollack (or other white firm-fleshed fish), skinned and pinboned

2 tbsp olive oil

2 onions, coarsely chopped

5cm piece fresh root ginger, peeled and finely grated

2 garlic cloves, crushed

2 tbsp hot curry powder

1 tsp ground coriander

1/2 tsp ground turmeric

1 x 400g tin chopped tomatoes

25g fresh coriander, leaves and stems separated

1 x 400ml tin coconut milk

1/2 lemon, juiced

mango chutney, to serve

salt and freshly cracked black pepper

1 Cut the fish into bite-sized chunks and refrigerate.

2 Heat the oil in a large non-stick frying pan and sweat the onions for 10 minutes, until softened. Add the ginger and garlic, stirring for another 2 minutes, before stirring in the curry powder, ground coriander and turmeric.

3 Stir in the tomatoes, coriander stems and coconut milk. Increase the heat and simmer for 15 minutes, until slightly thickened, adding a dash of lemon juice to taste.

4 Add the fish and cook for a further 5 minutes. Just before serving, season well and add a sprinkling of fresh coriander leaves. Serve immediately with rice and mango chutney or mango salsa (see p. 145) or kachumba (see p. 143).

Baked Salmon Parcels

Serves 4

The culinary term for these parcels is 'en papillote'. Let your guests unwrap the parcels at the table so they can delight in the wonderful aromas as they unfold.

4 x 150g salmon fillets, skinned and pinboned

4 spring onions, sliced at an angle

2cm fresh root ginger, cut into fine matchsticks

25g butter, cubed

4 tsp dry white wine

1 lemon, cut into wedges

salt and freshly cracked black pepper

Preheat the oven to 170°C/325°F/gas mark 3.

1 Cut out four 25cm x 25cm squares of parchment paper. Place each fish fillet on a separate square.

2 Divide the spring onions, ginger and butter between the squares and season with salt and pepper.

3 Just before baking, add 1 tsp of wine to each parcel, fold the paper over the fish and tuck in the edges to create 4 sealed parcels. Place on a baking sheet and bake in the oven for 10–12 minutes.

4 Serve with a wedge of lemon.

Thai Red Monkfish Curry

Serves 4

Thai food is all about balancing flavours. In the school, we can never agree on how much coconut milk to add, as everyone likes it made the way it is done in their favourite Thai restaurant.

100g baby corn cobs, sliced in half lengthways

1 tbsp red curry paste

300ml coconut milk

100ml fish stock (see p. 192)

200g button mushrooms

1/2 yellow pepper, deseeded and sliced into strips

1–2 tbsp fish sauce, to taste

1 tbsp lime juice

3 makrut lime leaves, deveined and torn

400g monkfish tail, skinned and cut into thick medallions

1 red chilli, sliced diagonally, to garnish

2 spring onions, cut on the diagonal, to garnish

1 Blanch the baby corn cobs in boiling water for 2 minutes. Refresh under cold water, drain and set aside.

2 Put the red curry paste into a wok or large non-stick pan and cook for 2 minutes (if it starts to spit, add a splash of the coconut milk). Add the coconut milk and fish stock and bring to the boil before adding the mushrooms and yellow pepper. Simmer for about 8 minutes, until the vegetables have softened.

3 Add the fish sauce, lime juice and lime leaves. Taste the sauce at this stage and adjust the flavours to your taste (add more lime juice if you find the sauce too salty or too fiery hot).

4 Add the monkfish medallions and baby corn cobs. Simmer for a further 6–8 minutes, until the monkfish is cooked.

5 Garnish with sliced red chillies and spring onions and serve with rice.

MAKRUT LIMES YIELD LITTLE JUICE, BUT THEIR LEAVES ARE HIGHLY AROMATIC AND ARE USED EXTENSIVELY IN SOUTH-EAST ASIAN COOKING. IF YOU CAN'T FIND THEM IN THE SHOPS, SUBSTITUTE SOME LIME ZEST AND JUICE.

Seared Tuna Steaks with Avocado Salsa

Serves 4

Tuna steaks are best served rare (a little pink in the middle), otherwise the flesh will be dry and the colour will be grey and unappetising.

4 x 150g tuna steaks (approximately 1.5cm thick)

1–2 tbsp olive oil

2 tbsp crème fraîche

salt and freshly cracked black pepper

AVOCADO SALSA

2 large avocadoes, peeled and cut into small chunks

1 lime, juiced

4 large vine tomatoes, deseeded and diced

¹/₂ red onion, very finely chopped

¹/₂ red chilli, deseeded and finely chopped

2 tbsp good-quality extra virgin olive oil

3–4 drops Tabasco sauce

10g fresh coriander, leaves chopped

salt and freshly cracked black pepper

1 To make the salsa, place the diced avocado in a bowl with a squeeze of lime juice (to stop the flesh discolouring). Add the tomatoes, red onion, chilli, olive oil and Tabasco sauce. Add seasoning and more lime juice to taste. Lastly, stir through the chopped coriander leaves.

2 Pat the tuna steaks dry with kitchen paper, rub a little olive oil over each steak and season both sides with salt and pepper.

3 Heat a large heavy-based frying plan. When very hot, first test a small piece of tuna and sear for 1–2 minutes on each side (removing from the heat when a middle layer of pink is still visible up the sides). Sear the 4 steaks together in the hot frying pan.

4 Serve immediately on a bed of avocado salsa, garnished with a dollop of crème fraîche.

RUBBING OIL OVER THE SURFACE OF THE TUNA STEAKS MEANS THAT YOU WON'T NEED TO ADD OIL TO THE FRYING PAN.

Pan-Fried Teriyaki Salmon

Serves 4

4 x 175g salmon fillets, skinned
  and pinboned

1 tbsp sunflower oil

MARINADE:

100ml light soy sauce

100ml saké

100ml mirin

2 tbsp caster sugar

1 Mix all the marinade ingredients in a bowl, then add the salmon fillets. Refrigerate and leave to marinate overnight (or for at least 20 minutes).

2 Remove the salmon from the marinade, pat dry with kitchen paper and set aside.

3 Simmer the liquid until it's reduced by half.

4 Heat the oil over a medium-high heat in a heavy-based frying pan. Fry the salmon, presentation side down first, for 3–4 minutes on each side (depending upon their thickness), until the salmon just turns opaque but is still moist or pink in the middle.

5 Pour the reduced liquid over the salmon and serve with a julienne salad of carrot, cucumber and mint (see p. 46).

SAKÉ IS A JAPANESE ALCOHOLIC DRINK (IT IS OFTEN REFERRED TO AS RICE WINE). IT HAS MANY COOKING PURPOSES AND IS COMMONLY USED TO TENDERISE, TONE DOWN SALTINESS AND TAME FISHY FLAVOURS IN DISHES.

Sea Bass Bouillabaisse

Serves 4

For a dinner party, I like to make the broth first and leave poaching the fish until the very last minute.

4 fillets sea bass, skin on and scaled

BROTH

750ml fish stock (see p. 192) (if not available, use a good-quality vegetable stock)

100ml white wine

$^1/_2$ orange, zest and juice

pinch saffron (approximately 15 strands)

1 tbsp olive oil

30g butter

1 onion, finely sliced

2 carrots, peeled and sliced into 2mm-thin discs

1 leek, cut diagonally into 5cm lengths

1 fennel bulb, trimmed, quartered and sliced

4 stalks celery, cut into chunks

3 tomatoes, roughly chopped

2 tsp fresh herbs (finely chopped chives and flat leaf parsley), to serve

croutons or crusty bread, to serve

salt and freshly cracked black pepper

1 In a small saucepan, heat the stock and add the wine, orange zest and juice and saffron. Remove from the heat and leave to infuse for a few minutes.

2 In a large non-stick pan, heat the oil and half the butter over a medium heat and sweat the onion and carrots for approximately 5 minutes, until soft but not coloured.

3 Add the rest of the butter, leek, fennel, celery and tomatoes and continue cooking for another 10 minutes. Season well.

4 Add the hot stock to the vegetables. Check for seasoning and simmer for 15 minutes, until the vegetables are softened.

5 Using a sharp knife, score the skin of each sea bass fillet twice and season (if the fillets are large, it's a good idea to cut them in half and serve the 2 halves overlapping). Cover the pan and poach the fillets in the simmering broth (skin side facing up) for 6–8 minutes, depending on the size of the fillets (it's cooked when you see the flesh turn opaque through the scored skin and it flakes easily).

6 Divide the vegetables between 4 wide bowls, place the sea bass on top and ladle the hot broth into each bowl. Garnish with finely chopped herbs and serve with crispy croutons.

A BROTH OF FISH STOCK, SAFFRON, FENNEL AND ORANGE, A BOUILLABAISSE CAN BE ADAPTED BY USING DIFFERENT FISH AND SHELLFISH.

Crispy Baked Cod

Serves 4

An easy, tasty and nutritious dinner dish.

4 x 150g fillets of cod (or haddock or salmon), skinned and pinboned

2 tbsp Dijon mustard

salt and freshly cracked black pepper

CRUMB TOPPING

25g flaked almonds

8 tbsp breadcrumbs

2 spring onions, finely sliced

20g parsley, finely chopped

2 tbsp olive oil (or melted butter)

Preheat the oven to 180°C/350°F/gas mark 4.

1 To make the crumb topping, line a baking sheet with tin foil and roast the flaked almonds for 4 minutes. Set aside and allow the baking sheet to cool (it will be used for the fish). Mix together the remaining topping ingredients and set aside.

2 Pat the fish dry, season and place on the baking sheet. Spread 1 tsp of Dijon mustard over the top of each fish fillet. Spoon the crumb topping evenly over the surface of each piece of fish.

3 Increase the oven temperature to 200°C/400°F/gas mark 6 and bake the fish for 12–15 minutes (depending on the thickness of the fish) and until the breadcrumbs are golden brown.

4 Serve with French beans, boiled new potatoes, roast tomatoes (see p. 92) or salad.

Fish Pie

Serves 4

2 eggs

1kg (or 6 medium) floury
potatoes, peeled and cut in half

50ml milk, hot

100g butter

150ml white wine (or fish stock,
see p. 192)

150ml water

1 large carrot, peeled and cut
into bite-sized diagonal chunks

1 bouquet garni (bay, thyme,
parsley)

3 sprigs fresh dill (separate the
sprigs and leaves)

550g fish, skinned and pinboned
(mixture of 250g salmon, 200g
haddock, 100g smoked cod),
cut into chunks

150ml cream

2 tbsp flour

100g cooked medium-sized
prawns

pinch freshly grated nutmeg

salt and freshly cracked black
pepper

Preheat the oven to 190°C/375°F/gas mark 5.

1 Place the eggs in a saucepan of water. Bring to the boil, then simmer for 7 minutes. Remove from the heat and run under cold water before shelling. Cut into quarters.

2 Steam the potatoes for 15–20 minutes, until they can be pierced easily with a fork. Mash with the milk and 75g of the butter. Set aside.

3 Heat the wine and water in a medium saucepan. Add the carrot, bouquet garni and dill sprigs. Season well and bring to the boil, then add the fish and poach for 3 minutes. Strain the liquid into a jug and add the cream.

4 Carefully transfer the fish and carrot to an ovenproof dish, discarding the bouquet garni and dill sprigs.

5 Wipe the poaching saucepan clean, melt the remaining 25g butter in the saucepan and stir in the flour to form a paste. Cook the paste for 2 minutes before gradually adding the creamy stock, stirring well until you have a smooth, thickened sauce.

6 Add the prawns, eggs and dill leaves to the dish before pouring in the sauce.

7 Place spoonfuls of mash over the filling, then gently join the small mounds of mash together with a knife or the back of a spoon (spread the mash to the edges of the dish, otherwise the sauce will bubble up and spill over). Grate over some nutmeg and cook in the oven for 30–40 minutes. For a golden crust, place the dish under a grill for the last few minutes.

....

A VELOUTÉ SAUCE IS A BASIC FRENCH SAUCE MADE WITH STOCK. IT GETS ITS NAME FROM ITS VELVETY TEXTURE AND IS OFTEN ENRICHED AT THE END WITH AN EGG YOLK AND A LITTLE CREAM.

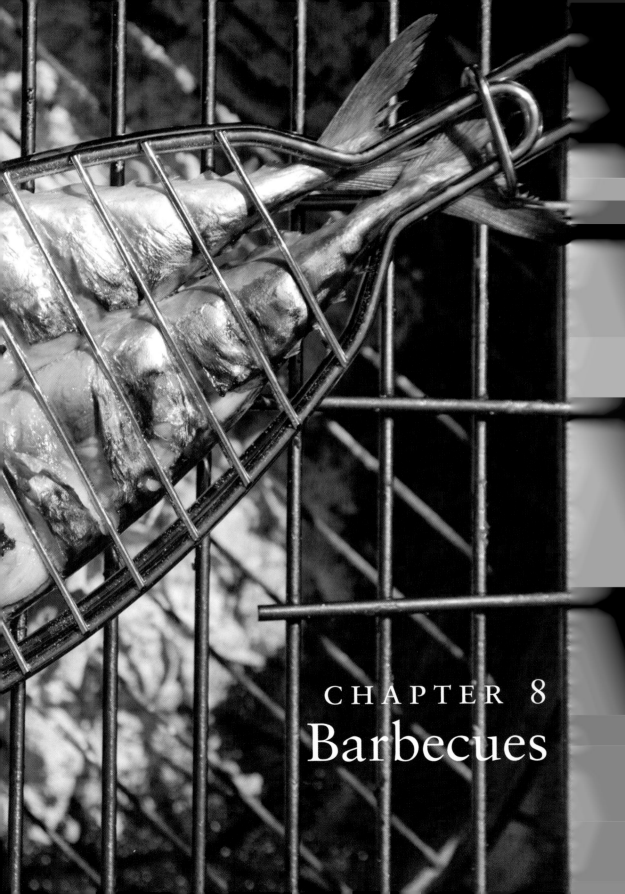

CHAPTER 8

Barbecues

Barbecue Glazed Chicken

Serves 4

6 dried apricots (presoaked, ready to eat), roughly chopped

3 tbsp boiling water

1 tbsp dark brown sugar (or muscovado sugar)

3 tbsp Worcestershire sauce

1 tbsp fresh ginger, grated

1 clove garlic, crushed

4 drops Tabasco sauce

1 tbsp olive oil

1 tbsp tomato purée

4 chicken breasts, cut into bite-sized pieces

1 red pepper, deseeded and cut into 2cm cubes

1 red onion, cut into 2cm cubes

1 yellow pepper, deseeded and cut into 2cm cubes

3 sprigs fresh parsley, roughly chopped

salt and freshly cracked black pepper

1 Combine the apricots, water, sugar, Worcestershire sauce, ginger, garlic, Tabasco sauce, olive oil and tomato purée in a saucepan and simmer for 5 minutes. Whiz with a handheld blender and season to taste. Transfer half the sauce to a medium bowl and add the chicken. Refrigerate and leave to marinate for 1 hour, until ready to barbecue.

2 Thread the red pepper, chicken, onion, yellow pepper (repeating in this order) onto long skewers. Brush with olive oil and season.

3 Heat the barbecue until very hot. Grill the skewers for 10 minutes, turning occasionally for even cooking. Brush the reserved glaze generously over the skewers and continue grilling for another few minutes until slightly caramelised. Continue basting with the glaze.

4 Once the chicken is cooked through, serve on a platter and scatter with freshly chopped parsley.

IF USING BAMBOO SKEWERS, PRESOAK THEM IN COLD WATER FOR 1 HOUR. THIS WILL PREVENT THEM FROM BURNING.

Warm Chargrilled Vegetable Salad

Serves 4

Vegetarians will be handsomely catered for at your barbecue with this delicious salad.

1 red pepper, deseeded and quartered

1 yellow pepper, deseeded and quartered

10–15 asparagus spears

1 courgette, sliced diagonally into 1cm-thick discs

1 tbsp olive oil

2 tbsp good-quality extra virgin olive oil

15g flat leaf parsley, leaves chopped

10g fresh basil, leaves only

salt and freshly cracked black pepper

1 Heat the barbecue until it's very hot. Grill the peppers skin side down until the outer skin is blackened and blistered. Place in a bowl, cover immediately with cling film and leave for 20 minutes (the cling film will trap the steam and loosen the skins). Peel the peppers, discarding the skin, and slice lengthways into 3–4 long strips (the strips will be deliciously soft and sweet).
2 Snap off the hard woody ends from each asparagus spear (if necessary).
3 Brush the asparagus and courgette with olive oil and season with salt and pepper. Grill for approximately 5–10 minutes, turning halfway through cooking until slightly charred on the outside. Cut the asparagus spears in half.
4 Combine all the warm vegetables in a bowl and toss in the extra virgin olive oil and add the chopped herbs. Serve warm or at room temperature.

Homemade Hamburgers

Serves 4

500g round steak, minced

1 onion, finely chopped

2 tsp English mustard

2 tsp Worcestershire sauce

½ tsp Tabasco sauce

25g flat leaf parsley, finely chopped

5 sprigs thyme, leaves only (or 2 sprigs rosemary)

10g chives, finely chopped

1 egg, lightly whisked

salt and freshly cracked black pepper

1 In a large, wide mixing bowl, first mix together the minced beef, onion, mustard, Worcestershire and Tabasco sauces (it's handy to wear gloves for this). Mix in the herbs and season well.

2 Lastly add the egg and mix thoroughly to bind the mixture.

3 Before shaping the hamburgers, fry a tiny piece of mince in a frying pan to check that the seasoning is to your liking. Adjust if necessary.

4 Shape the hamburgers into 2cm-thick patties (avoid making them too large or you risk undercooking them).

5 Cover and refrigerate the burgers until ready to cook.

6 Heat the barbecue until it's very hot. Brush the burgers lightly with oil and cook them for approximately 8–10 minutes on each side.

DO A HALF TURN ON EACH SIDE WHILE COOKING TO GIVE A CRISS-CROSS EFFECT.

Chargrilled Mackerel with Kachumba

Serves 4

Kachumba is something I love to eat with curry. It also goes well with grilled fish.

4 mackerel, gutted and cleaned

2 tbsp olive oil

1 lemon, cut into wedges, to serve

salt and freshly cracked black pepper

KACHUMBA

1 apple, cored and chopped

1 tbsp lemon juice

4 tomatoes, roughly chopped

$\frac{1}{2}$ cucumber, deseeded and roughly chopped

1 red onion, roughly chopped

salt and freshly cracked black pepper

1 To make the kachumba, toss the apple in the lemon juice and add the tomatoes, cucumber and red onion. Coat in olive oil and season to taste.

2 With a sharp knife, score two deep cuts down each side of the mackerel. Brush the mackerel with oil and season with salt and pepper.

3 Heat the barbecue until it's very hot. Place the whole fish in a metal fish grill and grill for 5-10 minutes on each side.

4 Serve with a spoonful of kachumba and a wedge of lemon on the side.

USE A LONG METAL FISH SLICE FOR TURNING FISH ON THE GRILL.

HALOUMI IS A HARD, SALTY SHEEP'S MILK CHEESE
THAT LENDS ITSELF TO GRILLING BECAUSE IT
DOENS'T MELT TOO EASILY.

Haloumi Cheese Skewers

Serves 4

To prepare these in advance indoors, you can fry them on a very hot pan until golden on the outside. Quickly reheat over the barbecue for that gorgeous smoky flavour.

250g haloumi cheese

2 tbsp olive oil

10 mint leaves, finely chopped

CAPER DRESSING

2 tbsp extra virgin olive oil

1 lime, zest and juice

1 tbsp baby capers

2 small pickled gherkins, sliced finely into discs

salt and freshly cracked black pepper

1 Mix the dressing ingredients together, season to taste and add more oil if necessary. Set aside.

2 Slice the haloumi into 2cm-thick slices. Brush both sides with oil.

3 Heat the barbecue until it's very hot and grill the haloumi slices for 1 minute on each side (remove them the moment the haloumi starts to melt). Once grilled, allow to cool slightly before cutting (or tearing) the haloumi into large bite-sized pieces and tossing in the dressing.

4 Just before serving, thread pieces of haloumi onto skewers. Place on a platter and garnish with the chopped mint.

Mango Salsa

Serves 4

A wonderful zesty, zingy salsa which is a perfect complement to the smoky flavours of the barbecued food.

2 tsp caster sugar

2 limes, zest and juice

2 mangoes, peeled and diced small

1 cucumber, peeled, deseeded and diced small

1 red chilli, finely chopped

5g mint, leaves chopped

5g coriander, leaves chopped

salt and freshly cracked black pepper

1 Stir the sugar into the lime juice until fully dissolved.

2 In a separate bowl, mix together the mango, cucumber, chilli and herbs.

3 Stir in the lime juice and zest and season to taste.

....

MAKE THE SALSA UP TO 3 HOURS IN ADVANCE. COVER WITH CLING FILM AND REFRIGERATE.

Caramelised Pineapple Wedges with Warm Chocolate Sauce

Serves 4

Other fruits such as mangoes and nectarines are also delicious grilled in this way. (Buy them slightly under-ripe!)

1 pineapple, tops cut off, cut into 4 wedges

sunflower oil

pinch caster sugar (as required)

CHOCOLATE SAUCE

100g dark chocolate, very finely chopped

100ml double cream

1 To make the sauce, heat the cream in a small pan to just below boiling point. Place the chopped chocolate in a bowl and add the hot cream. Leave to sit for 30 seconds before stirring slowly to a velvety smooth consistency (the sauce can be kept warm in a bain marie until ready to use).

2 Cut the pineapple lengthways, first in half, then into sixths or eighths. Slice away the core from the length of each wedge and brush lightly with unscented oil (sunflower oil is fine).

3 Heat the barbecue until it's hot. Grill the pineapple wedges on each side for 5 minutes, turning halfway through to create a criss-cross pattern.

4 Remove from the barbecue grid when they are slightly tender and nicely caramelised on the outside (sprinkling with a pinch of caster sugar will help them caramelise quicker). Serve next to a bowl of hot chocolate sauce so your guests can help themselves.

CLEAN THE GRILL WELL BEFORE GRILLING THE PINEAPPLE.

CHAPTER 9 Desserts

White Chocolate and Raspberry Cheesecake

Serves 6

180g ginger nut biscuits

50g butter, melted

400g good-quality cream cheese

60g caster sugar

$\frac{1}{2}$ lemon, zest and juice

300g good-quality white
chocolate, chopped

300ml cream, stiffly whipped

250g fresh raspberries

1 Crush the biscuits in a plastic bag with a rolling pin until they resemble breadcrumbs (this can also be done in a food processor). Stir the melted butter thoroughly into the biscuits. Press into the base of a greased 20cm loose-bottom cake tin (or springform tin) and chill in the fridge for 10 minutes to harden the base.

2 Using an electric mixer (or electric whisk), beat together the cream cheese, sugar, lemon zest and juice until smooth.

3 Melt the white chocolate in a bain marie (heatproof bowl set over a saucepan of barely simmering water). Once melted, slowly pour it into the beaten ingredients, whisking as you do so. Fold in the whipped cream.

4 To assemble the cheesecake, scatter half the raspberries over the base and pour half the filling over. Repeat with the remaining raspberries and filling and level the top with the back of a spoon. Leave to chill in the fridge for 4 hours or overnight.

5 Carefully remove from the tin and serve in wedges with a fruit coulis (see p. 193).

IF USING A SPRINGFORM TIN, DIP A PALETTE KNIFE IN HOT WATER AND RUN IT AROUND THE INSIDE OF THE TIN BEFORE RELEASING THE SPRING FOR A SMOOTHER EDGE.

Chocolate Biscuit Terrine

Makes 1 terrine

This is a popular alternative to the traditional wedding cake. It freezes brilliantly, so it can be made well in advance. You can also pack in whole hazelnuts, pistachios or raisins. For kids, some squidgy marshmallows are great fun.

170g unsalted butter

225g dark chocolate (75% cocoa solids), roughly chopped

25g caster sugar

25g cocoa powder

5 tbsp golden syrup

250g digestive biscuits

1 Line a 900g (2lb) loaf tin with parchment paper, allowing extra around the sides (for folding over later).

2 In a medium saucepan, melt the butter and chocolate over a low heat, stirring continuously. When fully melted, stir in the sugar, cocoa powder and golden syrup.

3 Break the biscuits into 2cm chunks and place in a bowl. Pour half the melted chocolate over the biscuits and stir carefully to coat.

4 Press a layer of biscuit mixture into the tin, then pour over a layer of melted chocolate (ensure the chocolate seeps down through the gaps). Repeat with the remaining biscuits and chocolate.

5 Flatten the top layer with the back of a spoon and fold over the parchment paper to cover the top. Set aside to cool before placing in the fridge for 4 hours (or overnight) to set fully.

6 To serve, remove from the fridge, peel away the paper and cut into slices with a knife dipped in boiling hot water.

POURING BOILING WATER OVER THE SPOON BEFORE DIPPING IT INTO THE TIN OF GOLDEN SYRUP WILL HELP THE SYRUP GLIDE OFF THE SPOON.

Plum Pâtisseries

Serves 4

These delicate French pâtisseries couldn't be easier. Try other fruits, such as apples, pears, apricots or peaches.

225g pre-rolled all butter puff pastry

2–3 plums, stoned, halved and sliced

15g butter, melted

2 tsp caster sugar

1 tbsp redcurrant jelly (or black-currant jam)

dash lemon juice

100g cream, freshly whipped

Preheat the oven to 200°C/400°F/gas mark 6.

1 Unfold the pastry. If not already rolled, roll out to a 2mm thickness.

2 To create a rim which will rise during cooking, use the rim of a wine glass to lightly score 4 circular imprints in the pastry (without cutting through the pastry). With the tip of a sharp knife, create an outer circle around the central one, but this time cutting through the pastry. Peel the pastry discs away from the pastry and transfer onto a baking sheet lined with parchment paper, then prick the inner circles of pastry several times with a fork (this will stop them puffing up too much in the oven).

3 Arrange overlapping slices of plum inside the inner circle and brush all over with melted butter. Sprinkle $\frac{1}{2}$ tsp of caster sugar over the fruit (otherwise the plums can be quite tart once cooked).

4 Bake in the oven for 15 minutes, until the pastry is puffed and golden. Set aside to cool.

5 Heat the redcurrant jelly and lemon juice in a small pan, until melted (loosen with a little water if necessary). Brush the warm glaze over the top of each patisserie and serve with freshly whipped cream.

Chocolate Roulade

Serves 6 to 8

A flourless dessert which tastes even better if made the day before a dinner party!

200g plain chocolate (75% cocoa solids), roughly chopped

5 eggs, separated into whites and yolks

140g caster sugar

sunflower oil, for greasing the tin

1 tbsp icing sugar, sieved

200ml cream, lightly whipped

100g raspberries, some for filling and some to decorate the plate

Preheat the oven to 200°C/400°F/gas mark 6.

1 Melt the chocolate in a bain marie (a bowl set over a saucepan of simmering water). Remove from the heat and leave to cool.

2 Using an electric whisk, beat the egg yolks and the caster sugar for a few minutes, until thick and pale (mousse-like). Fold in the melted chocolate until marbled looking.

3 Whisk the egg whites until stiff peaks form and stir a large metal spoonful into the chocolate mixture to loosen it. Gently fold the remaining whites into the chocolate mixture. Spread the mixture evenly onto a Swiss roll tin lined with parchment paper and bake for 15 minutes, until the top is springy to the touch. Leaving the sponge in the tin, cover immediately with a clean damp cloth (to prevent the sponge from cracking) until cool.

4 Lay a sheet of parchment paper on a work surface and dust with some icing sugar. Remove the cloth and turn out the sponge onto the parchment paper, peeling away the original paper.

5 Fold half the icing sugar into the whipped cream, then spread it evenly over the sponge. Scatter over most of the raspberries.

6 Starting with the long edge closest to you, roll the sponge up and over. Place the roulade onto a serving dish and dust with extra icing sugar and decorate with any remaining berries.

BRUSHING A LITTLE UNSCENTED OIL OVER THE TIN BEFORE PRESSING THE PARCHMENT PAPER INTO THE TIN HELPS THE PAPER TO MOULD TO THE SHAPE OF THE TIN.

Pear Frangipane Tart

Serves 6

This is an absolute classic for quick entertaining. If you are making your own shortcrust pastry, roll it out, line the tin and freeze, to keep one step ahead in your party preparations.

225g pre-rolled all butter short-crust pastry (or see p. 190)

100g butter, softened

100g caster sugar

1 egg, beaten

1 egg yolk

100g ground almonds

1 x 400g tinned pear halves, drained (or very ripe pears, peeled and halved)

3 tbsp apricot jam

1 tbsp lemon juice

Preheat the oven to 180°C/350°F/gas mark 4.

1 Grease a 20cm loose-bottomed flan tin. Place the shortcrust pastry in the bottom to cover it.

2 Using an electric whisk, cream the butter and sugar until pale and fluffy. Add the egg and yolk slowly to prevent the mixture from curdling, then mix in the ground almonds until you have a thick paste. Spoon into the flan case and spread out evenly. Refrigerate for 10 minutes to harden up slightly.

3 Without cutting through the top, slice each pear half lengthways and splay out to give a fan effect. Carefully arrange the fans over the top of the filling. Place the tart on a hot baking sheet and bake in the oven for 30 minutes (check after 15 minutes and if the top is browning, turn the oven down to 170°C/325°F/gas mark 3). Remove from the oven and leave to cool.

4 Heat the apricot jam in a small pan with the lemon juice. Pass through a sieve (and loosen with a little water if necessary). Brush the warm glaze over the top of the tart and serve either warm or cold.

IT'S IMPORTANT TO ENSURE THE TART BASE IS COOKED. IN THE SCHOOL, WE PUT IT IN THE OVEN ON A HOT BAKING TRAY.

Citrus Fruit Salad

Serves 4

Make up a larger quantity of sugar syrup (without the lime) and it will keep in the fridge for a month. Add lemon juice to make fresh lemonade.

2 oranges

1 blood orange

1 pink or ruby grapefruit

1 tsp Cointreau (or Grand Marnier)

SUGAR SYRUP

50g sugar

50ml water

1 lime, zest and juice

1 Make the sugar syrup by dissolving the sugar in the water over a low heat. Once the sugar is fully dissolved, bring to the boil (without stirring) and simmer for 5 minutes, until syrupy.

2 Add the lime juice and zest while the syrup is still warm. Set aside to cool and refrigerate.

3 Segment the citrus fruits using a small sharp knife, removing the peel, pith and skin.

4 Place the segmented fruit in a serving bowl. Stir in the liqueur and syrup.

5 Cover and chill until needed. Remove from the fridge 30 minutes before serving.

STIRRING AFTER THE SUGAR BOILS CAUSES CRYSTALS TO FORM. IF THE SYRUP SPLASHES, BRUSH THE INSIDE OF THE PAN WITH COLD WATER OR DAMP KITCHEN PAPER.

Chocolate Mousse

Serves 6

Another way to serve this is in the centre of a buffet table in a beautiful crystal bowl (if teamed with other desserts, it will provide 10 servings).

250g dark chocolate (75% cocoa solids)

6 eggs

150g caster sugar

1 tbsp freshly brewed coffee

mint leaves, to decorate

1 Break the chocolate into small pieces and melt in a bain marie (a heatproof bowl set over a saucepan of barely simmering water). Remove from the heat and leave to cool.

2 Separate the egg yolks from the whites and put the yolks and whites into 2 separate bowls.

3 Beat the yolks with the sugar until pale and mousse-like (the sugar should be fully dissolved). Mix in the coffee, then stir in the melted chocolate until fully combined.

4 Whisk the egg whites until they form stiff peaks. Stir 1 spoonful of whites into the chocolate mixture to loosen it, then carefully fold in the remaining whites using a cutting and folding motion, until well combined.

5 Pour the mousse into ramekins (or martini glasses or espresso cups). Chill in the fridge for 2 hours and serve decorated with fresh mint leaves.

WHEN FOLDING IN THE EGG WHITES, USE A CUTTING AND FOLDING MOTION SO THAT ALL THE CHOCOLATE MIXTURE FROM THE BASE OF THE BOWL GETS MIXED IN. HOWEVER, KEEP THE MIXTURE LIGHT BY FOLDING GENTLY.

Baked Cheesecake

Serves 6 to 8

The yoghurt topping on this cheesecake is great with the sweet filling.

140g digestive biscuits

60g butter, melted

300g good-quality cream cheese

160g caster sugar

3 eggs

3 tbsp lemon juice

$^1/_2$ tsp vanilla essence

YOGHURT TOPPING

120ml natural yoghurt (pouring consistency)

1 tsp caster sugar

$^1/_2$ tsp vanilla essence

Preheat the oven to 180°C/350°F/gas mark 4.

1 Crush the biscuits in a plastic bag with a rolling pin until they resemble breadcrumbs. Stir the melted butter thoroughly into the biscuits. Press into the base of a greased 20cm loose-bottom cake tin (or springform tin) and chill in the fridge for 10 minutes to harden the base.

2 Meanwhile, using an electric mixer, whisk together the cream cheese, sugar, eggs, lemon juice and vanilla essence to a smooth consistency.

3 Pour the mixture slowly over the biscuit base. Bake in the oven for 30 minutes, until the cheesecake no longer wobbles in the centre (if the surface of the cheesecake starts to brown, turn down the oven temperature).

4 Remove the cheesecake from the oven and leave to cool for 15 minutes.

5 To make the topping, stir together the yoghurt, caster sugar and vanilla essence and spread over the top of the cheesecake. Leave to cool in the fridge for at least 2 hours. Carefully remove from the tin and serve chilled.

YOU CAN ALSO CRUSH THE BISCUITS IN A FOOD PROCESSOR.

Strawberry Ripple Ice Cream

Serves 6

You don't need an ice cream maker to make wonderful ice cream.

500g frozen (or fresh) strawberries

$^1/_2$ lemon, juiced (about 2 tbsp)

200g caster sugar

300ml cream, lightly whipped

1 Place the strawberries in a food processor and lightly pulse the machine to roughly chop the berries. Remove half the strawberries and set aside in a bowl. Continue processing the remaining strawberries until smooth.

2 Add the lemon juice and sugar to the puréed strawberries, and continue processing until the sugar is fully dissolved. Combine well.

3 Transfer to a large bowl, add the roughly chopped strawberries and gently fold in the cream.

4 Pour into a 1 litre freezer-proof container and freeze for 1 hour to start. Remove from the freezer and stir vigorously with a whisk (to break up any ice crystals), then return to the freezer. Stir every half hour, repeating about 4 times, after which you can leave it in the freezer until ready to serve (alternatively, pour into a standard size ice cream maker and proceed as per instructions).

5 Before serving, remove from the freezer and allow to 'ripen' in the fridge for 10 minutes.

....

POPPING A FREEZER-PROOF CERAMIC CONTAINER IN THE FREEZER FOR 1 HOUR BEFORE ADDING THE ICE CREAM MIXTURE WILL HELP THE ICE CREAM FREEZE FASTER.

Meringues

Makes 12

Tim's mother makes the most wonderful gooey meringues and this is her recipe – a real family favourite.

4 egg whites, at room temperature

225g caster sugar

1/8 tsp salt

125ml cream, freshly whipped

Preheat the oven to 100°C/200°F/gas mark 1/4.

1 Whisk the egg whites to stiff peaks, then add half the sugar and the salt and continue to whisk until the mixture holds its shape and is glossy.

2 Gently fold in the remainder of the sugar with a clean metal spoon.

3 Line a baking sheet with parchment paper and pipe the mixture onto the tray with a piping bag (alternatively, use 2 wet dessertspoons and, from a height, drop a good dollop of the mixture onto the parchment paper and shape from around the edges, working from the base upwards and inwards and ending with a peaked swirl on the top (they will rise slightly).

4 Cook in the oven for 1 1/4–2 hours (if you like them slightly chewy in the middle, they will take a little less time). Remove from the oven and cool on a wire rack. Serve 2 meringues sandwiched together with freshly whipped cream or strawberry ripple ice cream (see p. 161).

TO SUCCESSFULLY WHISK EGG WHITES, USE CLEAN, GREASE-FREE EQUIPMENT AND AVOID EVEN THE SMALLEST SPECK OF EGG YOLK GETTING INTO THE EGG WHITES.

Flourless Apple and Blackberry Crumble

Serves 4

For a gluten-free version, try to source gluten-free porridge oats. Using a large pot to cook the apples will help keep their shape. Serve with some thick Crozier sheep's yoghurt as a change from whipped cream.

5 medium cooking apples,
  peeled, cored and cubed

125g golden caster sugar

1 tsp ground cinnamon

½ lemon, zest and juice

200g fresh blackberries

75g butter, chilled and cubed

4 tbsp honey

150g porridge oats

100g freshly whipped cream, to
  serve

Preheat the oven to 200°C/400°F/gas mark 6.

1 Place the apples in a large heavy-bottomed saucepan with 80g of the golden caster sugar, half the cinnamon and all the lemon zest and juice. Stir well to combine.

2 Cover and cook over a gentle heat for 10 minutes, stirring occasionally until the apples are just tender but still retain their shape. Adjusting to your desired sweetness, stir in the remaining golden caster sugar and cinnamon. Transfer the mixture to a 1.1 litre ovenproof dish and scatter over the blackberries, pressing them into the mixture until partially submerged.

3 Meanwhile, heat the butter and honey in a saucepan and cook on a high heat for 5 minutes. Mix in the oats to coat well.

4 Cover the filling with an even layer of oat crumble (the more crumble around the edges, the less liquid filling will spill over the sides). Place the dish on a baking sheet and bake in the oven for 20 minutes, or until the crumble is slightly toasted and the filling has started to bubble. Remove from the oven and serve warm with freshly whipped cream, custard or even yoghurt.

Grandma's Old-fashioned Rhubarb Pie

Serves 6

Stewed fruit freezes wonderfully (as does raw rhubarb). I always make double so that I can whip up a second pie when foul weather turns us indoors.

900g rhubarb, trimmed, washed and cut into chunks

150g golden caster sugar

1/2 lemon, zest and juice

225g self-raising flour

1/2 tsp table salt

110g butter, cubed small and chilled

1 egg, lightly whisked

a second egg, to glaze

1 heaped tsp granulated sugar

100ml cream, freshly whipped

Preheat the oven to 180°C/350°F/gas mark 4.

1 Put the rhubarb into a fairly large heavy-bottomed saucepan with the sugar and the lemon zest and juice. Cover and cook over a gentle heat for 10 minutes, until the rhubarb is just tender but still retains its shape. Strain and reserve the cooking liquid, return it to the saucepan and simmer until it is further reduced. Allow to cool.

2 Sieve the flour, sugar and salt into a bowl, then rub in the butter until the mixture resembles fine breadcrumbs. Using a knife to cut and stir, gradually mix in the egg to form a stiff paste. Bring the dough together with your hands into a ball and divide the pastry into 2 pieces. Wrap in cling film and chill for 20 minutes.

3 Turn 1 piece of dough onto a lightly floured work surface and roll out and line a greased 20cm pie dish. Add the cooled rhubarb filling and the reduced liquid. Roll out the second piece of pastry and cover the top of the pie with it.

4 Trim the loose edges with a knife and seal the pastry together by lightly pressing the back of a fork around the rim of the dish. Make 2 small slits in the centre of the pie (for the steam to escape) and use the pastry trimmings to create attractive decorative shapes (small leaves are easy). Brush the top of the pastry with the egg glaze and dredge with granulated sugar.

5 Bake in the oven for 30 minutes, until golden. Serve at room temperature (or warm) with whipped cream.

'FORCED' RHUBARB IS SPECIALLY CULTIVATED TO BE AVAILABLE EARLY IN THE SEASON. THE STALKS ARE BRIGHT PINK AND MORE TENDER THAN ORDINARY RHUBARB.

Lemon Tart

Serves 4–6

This citrus hit is a real family favourite and a winner in our Pastries and Desserts classes.

225g pre-rolled all butter short-crust pastry (or see p. 190)

3 unwaxed lemons

170g caster sugar

4 eggs

125ml cream

Preheat the oven to 180°C/350°F/gas mark 4.

1 Roll the pastry out on a lightly floured work surface to a 2mm thickness. Line a greased 20cm loose-bottomed flan tin with the pastry, then prick several times with a fork. Cover the pastry with parchment paper and fill with baking beans. Bake for 20 minutes. Remove the beans and paper and return the pastry case to the oven for 5 more minutes, until it's a light golden colour.

2 Using a very fine grater, finely grate the zest from 2 of the lemons before squeezing the juice from all 3 (ensure that you are only grating the outer zest and not grating through to the white pith).

3 In a mixing bowl, combine the lemon zest, juice and sugar. Stir until the sugar is fully dissolved.

4 Break up the eggs with a whisk.

5 Add the eggs and cream to the lemon mixture. Mix well with an electric whisk (or vigorously with a balloon whisk). Skim off any excess foam.

6 Pour into the baked pastry base. Bake in the oven for 25 minutes, until the filling is firm in the centre (when you shake the tin, the filling should no longer wobble in the centre).

IF YOU DON'T HAVE CERAMIC BAKING BEANS, USE A PACKET OF RAW DRIED KIDNEY BEANS (OR LENTILS), WHICH CAN BE REUSED FOR BAKING BLIND UNTIL THEY DRY OUT.

CHAPTER 10 Baking

Chocolate Caramel Squares

Makes 20

These biscuits are loved by all in the school. Using dark chocolate with 75% cocoa solids will offset the sweetness of the caramel, but use any dark chocolate you have handy.

220g butter, cubed, room temperature

100g caster sugar

350g plain flour, sifted

1 tbsp milk, if necessary

175g dark chocolate (minimum 55% cocoa solids)

CARAMEL

110g butter

75g granulated sugar

1 x 397g tin condensed milk

1 tbsp golden syrup

Preheat the oven to 170°C/325°F/gas mark 3.

1 For the shortbread, using an electric mixer (or electric whisk), cream the butter and sugar. Add the flour and continue beating until the mixture resembles fine breadcrumbs (this takes less than 1 minute if using an electric whisk). Add a small amount of milk only if necessary to bind the dough. Press the dough to a 1cm thickness into a greased baking tray. Bake in the oven for 25 minutes, or until pale golden.

2 For the caramel, melt the butter and sugar in a saucepan, stirring. When the sugar has dissolved fully, add the condensed milk and golden syrup. Increase the heat and bring the sauce to the boil. At this stage, stand over the pan and keep stirring for 20 minutes, until it turns a golden caramel colour (reduce the temperature if the sugar starts to catch on the base).

3 When the shortbread is cooked, allow it to cool for 10 minutes, then spread the caramel evenly over the top. Set aside to cool fully.

4 Melt the chocolate in a bain marie (a bowl set over a saucepan of simmering water). Pour the chocolate over the caramel and refrigerate for at least 1 hour, until the chocolate hardens. Cut into 4cm x 4cm squares.

THIS CARAMEL IS COOKED TO THE 'SOFT BALL' STAGE - THE BEST WAY TO TEST THIS IS TO DROP 1 TSP OF THE CARAMEL INTO A CUP OF COLD WATER. IT SHOULD FORM A SOFT BALL THAT DOES NOT HARDEN FULLY IN THE WATER.

Sicilian Apricot Biscuits

Makes 18

This recipe was inspired by a visit to Cucina Caldesi in London. The recipe is so simple and is flourless, which makes these biscuits perfect for coeliacs.

2 eggs, whites only

170g caster sugar

170g ground almonds

1 tsp orange zest

1 tbsp amaretto liqueur (or 1 tsp almond essence)

icing sugar, for rolling

50ml apricot jam

Preheat the oven to 170°C/325°F/gas mark 3.

1 In a large bowl, beat the egg whites until they form stiff peaks.

2 Combine the sugar, ground almonds and orange zest and gently fold into the egg whites. Stir in the amaretto liqueur. You should end up with a smooth paste.

3 Dust your hands with icing sugar and roll the paste into balls (the balls should be smooth, so dust your hands with icing sugar again if the mixture becomes unmanageably sticky).

4 Press your thumb into the centre of each ball and fill with a blob of apricot jam. Place on a baking sheet lined with parchment paper and sieve more icing sugar over the biscuits.

5 Bake in the oven for 20 minutes, until golden. Cool on a wire rack.

Brown Scones

Makes 16

We always tell our students that the secret with scones is not to overwork the dough. Once it comes together, the lighter the touch, the lighter your scones will be. A well-floured work surface is important for rolling out the moist dough.

200g wholemeal brown flour

200g plain white flour

1 heaped tsp salt

1 level tsp bread soda

300ml buttermilk

1 egg, lightly whisked

porridge oats, to sprinkle over the top (optional)

Preheat the oven to 200°C/400°F/gas mark 6.

1 Sieve both flours, the salt and bread soda into a large, wide mixing bowl (any wheat flakes left in the sieve can be tipped into the bowl).

2 Make a well in the centre and pour in three-quarters of the buttermilk. Using a spatula, stir the liquid through the dry ingredients as quickly as possible, until just combined, drawing in the flour from the sides of the bowl as you stir. If you still have dry flour in the bottom of the bowl, pour in the remaining milk and stir again (the dough should come together without being too wet and sticky – add more flour if it's sloppy).

3 Prepare a very well-floured work surface and turn the dough out onto it. Shape it into a round cake and pat it flat to a 3cm thickness before cutting out rounds with a medium scone cutter.

4 Place the scones on a baking sheet lined with parchment paper and brush the egg over the top of each scone (you can sprinkle over porridge oats before they go into the oven, if you have them).

5 Bake in the oven for 20 minutes (large scones will take slightly longer to cook). Transfer to a wire rack to cool.

THE SCONE DOUGH SHOULD BE QUITE MOIST, SO IT'S IMPORTANT TO FLOUR THE WORK SURFACE VERY WELL SO THAT YOU CAN SHAPE THE DOUGH AND CUT OUT THE SCONES EASILY.

Fruity Flapjacks

Makes 16–20

Home-baked cookies are always much healthier than processed ones. These are bursting with vitality with all the dried fruits and seeds.

350g medium porridge oats

1 heaped tsp ground cinnamon

85g walnuts, roughly chopped (or hazelnuts)

80g raisins

50g dried cranberries

80g dried apricots, chopped very small

70g sunflower seeds

20g pumpkin seeds

200g butter

4 tbsp honey

250g brown sugar

Preheat the oven to 190°C/375°F/gas mark 5.

1. In a large bowl, mix together the oats, cinnamon, walnuts, raisins, cranberries, apricots, sunflower seeds and pumpkin seeds (the quantities are interchangeable).

2. Melt the butter and honey in a pan, then stir in the sugar until the sugar is fully dissolved. Bring to the boil and cook for 1–2 minutes, stirring until thickened into a smooth sauce. Add half the sauce to the dry ingredients, stir well, then add the remaining sauce and stir until fully combined.

3. Spoon the mixture evenly into a baking tray lined with parchment paper, smoothing the surface with the back of a spoon.

4. Bake for 15–18 minutes, until caramelised and brown around the edges. Leave to cool in the tin before cutting into squares.

WITH SO MUCH FRUIT IN THESE FLAPJACKS, I LIKE TO BAKE THE MIXTURE ON A HIGH HEAT IN THE OVEN SO THE MIXTURE WILL CARAMELISE AND HARDEN UP WHEN COOLED, WHICH MAKES THEM EASIER TO CUT INTO SQUARES.

Auntie Margaret's Boiled Cake

Old recipes are always the best. This recipe was given to me by my stepmother, Roberta, who in turn was given it by her Auntie Margaret. I always visit at 4 p.m., knowing this cake will be served with tea from a china cup. The secret ingredient to this moist fruit cake is most definitely the pineapple.

100g butter

225g caster sugar

1 x 425g tin crushed pineapple,
including the juice

1 x 450g tin mixed luxury fruit

1 ½ tsp mixed spice

2 large eggs, lightly beaten

250g self-raising flour

1 heaped tsp bread soda

1 tbsp whiskey (optional)

Preheat the oven to 180°C/350°F/gas mark 4.

1 Melt the butter in a medium saucepan, then add the sugar and stir for 5 minutes, or until the suger has dissolved.

2 Add the pineapple (including the juice), mixed fruit and mixed spice. Bring to the boil, then simmer uncovered for 10 minutes.

3 Transfer to a large bowl and allow to cool before stirring in the eggs. Sieve together the flour and bread soda and fold them into the fruit (add a little extra flour if the mixture is too moist). Pour the mixture into a lined 20cm loose-bottom cake tin and bake in the oven for 1 hour.

4 Reduce the heat to 160°C/325°F/gas mark 3 and continue baking for a further 20 minutes. Leave to cool in the tin (if you intend to store it for a few weeks, pour 1 tbsp of whiskey over the cracks in the surface). Store in an airtight container.

YOU CAN USE A VARIETY OF DIFFERENT CAKE TINS (LOOSE-BOTTOMED, SPRINGFORM OR SOLID-BASED). HOWEVER, IT'S WORTH MENTIONING THAT IF YOU USE A SOLID-BASED TIN, IT'S IMPORTANT TO LINE THE BASE AND SIDES WITH PARCHMENT PAPER SO THE CAKE DROPS OUT OF THE TIN EASILY.

Strawberry Shortbread

Makes 12

These delicate, crumbly biscuits make a cute dessert to serve with coffee.

220g butter, cubed, room
temperature

100g caster sugar

350g plain flour, sifted

1 tbsp milk, if necessary

100ml cream, whipped

10–15 strawberries, hulled and
quartered

icing sugar, to dust

....

THESE BISCUITS CAN
BE STORED IN AN
AIRTIGHT CONTAINER
FOR UP TO 5 DAYS.

Preheat the oven to 170°C/325°F/gas mark 3.

1 Using an electric mixer (or electric whisk), cream together the butter and sugar until pale and fluffy. Add the flour and continue mixing until the mixture resembles fine breadcrumbs (this takes less than 1 minute). Add a small amount of milk only if necessary to bind the dough.

2 Roll out the dough on a lightly floured work surface to a 5mm thickness.

3 Cut out shapes with a cookie cutter and place them on a baking sheet lined with parchment paper.

4 Bake in the oven for 15 minutes, or until pale golden. Transfer to a wire rack to cool. Once cool, sandwich 2 cookies together with whipped cream and strawberries. Dust with icing sugar before serving.

Chocolate Chip Cookies

Makes 12

I have been baking these biscuits tirelessly since I learned the recipe in my Home Economics class at school. Cadbury's Dairy Milk chocolate was absolutely essential in those days, but good-quality dark chocolate is widely available now. These cookies will be delicious whether you use milk, dark or even white chocolate.

100g butter, softened, at room temperature

100g caster sugar

125g self-raising flour

50g custard powder

75g good-quality dark chocolate, chopped into chunks

1 tbsp cold water (if necessary)

Preheat the oven to 180°C/350°F/gas mark 4.

1 Using an electric mixer (or electric whisk), cream together the butter and sugar until pale.

2 Sieve together the flour and custard powder and continue mixing them into the butter and sugar until the mixture is the consistency of fine breadcrumbs. Stir in the chocolate chunks. With your hands, bring the mixture together to a firm dough, adding the water only if necessary to bind the dough.

3 Using your hands, roll the dough into table tennis-sized balls. Arrange on 2 baking sheets lined with parchment paper (leave ample space between cookies, as they will spread outwards during cooking). Chill in the fridge for 10 minutes before baking.

4 Bake in the oven for 12–15 minutes, until slightly risen and golden. Once cooked, leave to cool slightly before transferring them with a palette knife to a wire rack.

YOU CAN ROLL THE MIXTURE INTO A THICK SAUSAGE, WRAP IT IN CLING FILM AND SAVE IT IN THE FREEZER. WHEN YOU WANT TO BAKE SOME COOKIES, SIMPLY REMOVE IT FROM THE FREEZER FOR HALF AN HOUR AND SLICE INTO THICK COINS USING A KNIFE DIPPED IN HOT WATER. BAKE AS NORMAL.

Chocolate Brownies

Makes 16

225g dark chocolate

115g butter, cubed, at room
temperature

250g caster sugar

2 tsp vanilla essence

4 eggs, lightly whisked

175g plain flour

1/2 tsp baking powder

1/4 tsp salt

115g walnuts, roughly chopped

Preheat the oven to 180°C/350°F/gas mark 4.

1 Melt the chocolate in a bain marie (a bowl set over a saucepan of simmering water). Allow to cool.

2 Using an electric mixer (or electric whisk), cream the butter and sugar until pale. Whisk in the cooled chocolate, vanilla essence and eggs.

3 Sieve together the flour, baking powder and salt and gently fold these, along with the walnuts, into the wet mixture.

4 Pour the mixture into a baking tray lined with parchment paper and bake for 30–35 minutes, until the top is crusty. Allow to cool in the tin for 10 minutes, then turn out onto a wire rack. Cut into squares and store in an airtight container for up to 3 days.

YOU WILL KNOW WHEN THE BROWNIES ARE COOKED
WHEN A SKEWER INSERTED INTO THE CENTRE COMES
OUT CLEAN.

White Yeast Bread

Makes 1 loaf

The enigmatic Ursula Ferrigno has delighted our students on many occasions with her wonderful bread-making workshops. Her kneading technique is a fabulous workout and what satisfaction our students get when they see their bread ballooning in front of their eyes.

450g strong white flour, plus extra for dusting

2 level tsp table salt

2 tsp caster sugar

2 tsp easy-blend or fast-action yeast

1 tbsp extra virgin olive oil

300ml water, tepid

1 egg, lightly whisked with milk

1 tbsp sesame seeds (or poppy seeds)

STRONG WHITE FLOUR IS MADE FROM WHEAT THAT IS HIGH IN GLUTEN. THE GLUTEN GIVES THE DOUGH ITS STRETCHY QUALITY WHEN KNEADED.

Preheat the oven to 220°C/425°F/gas mark 7.

1 In a large, wide mixing bowl, sieve the flour, salt, sugar and yeast. Make a well in the centre and pour in the olive oil and water. Work the liquid into the flour with a wooden spoon, then bring it all together into a soft, elastic dough with your hands. Turn the dough out onto a lightly floured work surface and knead for 10 minutes, using a pushing and stretching motion with the heel of your hand, until smooth and bouncy (if kneading with an electric dough hook, this will take 5 minutes). While kneading, add more flour to the work surface, if required, to keep the dough moving freely.

2 Put the ball of dough in a lightly oiled bowl and drape a clean, dry tea towel on top. Leave the dough to rise (it will double in size within 1–2 hours in a warm room away from any draughts).

3 Once it has risen, knock back the dough (lightly punch the dough to release some air) and knead again for 2 minutes. Leave to relax for 10 minutes.

4 Shape the bread into a whole round loaf or tear off pieces of dough to make rolls. (To make a plait, divide the dough into 3 equal pieces and roll each into equal sausage lengths. Join the 3 ends, pinch them together and tuck underneath. Working from alternate sides, bring each tail over into the centre to form a plait, tucking under the end.)

5 Transfer the shaped dough onto a greased baking sheet. Cover and leave for 1 hour, until risen once more. Dust the top with flour for a rustic loaf or carefully brush egg wash over the top and sprinkle with sesame seeds.

6 Bake for 10 minutes before turning the oven down to 180°C/350°F/gas mark 4 for the remaining 20 minutes.

7 Cool on a wire rack. For a soft crust, wrap in a clean, dry tea towel while cooling.

Wholemeal Treacle Bread

Makes 1 x 900g loaf

sunflower oil (or other
  unscented oil)

540g wholemeal brown flour

1 heaped tsp bread soda

¹/₄ tsp salt

1 tbsp treacle

400ml buttermilk

1 tbsp porridge oats, to sprinkle
  over the top (optional)

Preheat the oven to 200°C/400°F/gas mark 6.

1 Generously grease a 900g (2lb) loaf tin with sunflower oil.

2 In a large mixing bowl, mix together the wholemeal flour, bread soda and salt. Stir the dry ingredients very well (this is important to distribute the bread soda evenly).

3 Stir in the treacle and buttermilk, mixing quickly. (Don't worry if it is very wet and sloppy.) Pour into the greased loaf tin and sprinkle porridge oats over the top. Shake the tin once to settle the mixture.

4 Place in a hot oven for 10 minutes, then reduce the oven temperature to 180°C/350°F/gas mark 4 for a further 50 minutes. Remove the bread from the oven and leave to rest for 10 minutes (during this time, steam causes the loaf to contract, so you can turn it out of the tin more easily). For a crusty loaf, return the loaf to the oven, resting on its side, for another 10 minutes.

LITTLE THINGS MAKE A BIG DIFFERENCE! WASH THE MIXING BOWL AS SOON AS YOU HAVE FINISHED WITH IT OR THE WET FLOUR WILL HARDEN AND REQUIRE DOUBLE YOUR EFFORT LATER ON.

Breakfast Bran Muffins

Makes 12

This is our fat-free muffin recipe that is light and-non greasy to the touch. Many different flavours can be added, such as chopped banana or cinnamon and grated apple.

110g plain flour
110g wholemeal flour
1 heaped tsp bread soda
pinch salt
1 egg
150g brown sugar (demerara)
200ml milk
1/2 tsp vanilla essence
175ml fresh orange juice

Preheat the oven to 180°C/350°F/gas mark 4.

1 Sieve together the flours, bread soda and salt into a mixing bowl, tipping any wheat flakes left in the sieve into the bowl.

2 Using an electric mixer (or electric whisk), beat together the egg, sugar, milk, vanilla essence and orange juice until smooth.

3 Using a spatula, gradually fold the wet ingredients into the dry, mixing well (it will be quite wet and sloppy).

4 Grease a 12-cup muffin tray (or place paper muffin cases inside each hollow) and divide the mixture between the hollows, only half filling each hollow, as the muffins will rise.

5 Bake in the oven for 20–25 minutes, until nicely risen and firm in the centre.

6 Transfer the muffins to a wire rack to cool.

WHOLEMEAL FLOUR IS MADE FROM THE WHOLE OF THE WHEAT GRAIN. TO MAKE WHITE FLOUR THE BRAN (HUSK) AND WHEATGERM (EMBRYO) ARE REMOVED.

Blueberry Muffins

Makes 12

Bake these muffins ahead and freeze them. Zap them from frozen in the microwave on high for 1 minute for delicious muffins every day. Alternatively, the batter will keep in the fridge for up to 2 weeks, and you can experiment with other fruit such as bananas.

220g plain flour

pinch salt

1 heaped tsp bread soda

1 egg

150g brown sugar (demerara)

200ml milk

1/2 tsp vanilla essence

175ml sunflower oil

125g blueberries

Preheat the oven to 180°C/350°F/gas mark 4.

1 Sieve together the flour, salt and bread soda into a mixing bowl.

2 Using an electric mixer (or electric whisk), beat together the egg, sugar, milk, vanilla essence and oil until smooth.

3 Using a spatula, gradually fold the wet ingredients into the dry, mixing well (it will be quite wet and sloppy).

4 Fold in the blueberries.

5 Grease a 12-cup muffin tray (or place paper muffin cases inside each hollow) and divide the mixture between the hollows, only half filling each hollow, as the muffins will rise.

6 Bake in the oven for 20–25 minutes, until nicely risen and firm in the centre.

7 Transfer the muffins to a wire rack to cool.

CHAPTER 11 Basics

Shortcrust Pastry

Makes 250g pastry

Students flock to our Perfect Pastries and Desserts class for a masterclass in pastry making. It's very simple, we tell them: work quickly and keep everything nice and cool.

170g plain flour, sieved
pinch of salt
100g butter, cubed small, chilled
1–2 tbsp cold water

Preheat the oven to 190°C/375°F/gas mark 5.

By hand method:
1 Sieve together the flour and salt in a large bowl and add the chilled butter.
2 Rub the butter into the flour with your fingertips until you have a mixture that resembles breadcrumbs with no lumps of butter remaining (work quickly so that it doesn't become greasy).
3 Using a knife, stir in half the cold water to bind the dough (add more water as required).
4 Bring the dough into a ball using your hands. Wrap the dough in cling film and chill for 20 minutes.

Food processor method:
1 Put the flour, salt and butter in a food processor and pulse until the fat and flour are combined to a breadcrumb consistency. With the motor running, gradually add the water through the funnel until the dough comes together (add just enough water to bind it). Wrap the dough in cling film and chill for 20 minutes.

To bake pastry blind:
1 Roll out the pastry thinly on a lightly floured work surface. Place in a greased 20cm loose-bottomed flan tin, pressing the pastry into the shape of the tin, and prick with a fork. Place a sheet of parchment paper on top of the pastry and fill with ceramic baking beans. Place in the oven for 25 minutes, until the base is pale golden. Remove the beans and paper. The case is now ready for the filling to be added.

TO AVOID A PASTRY WITH CRACKS WHERE THE FILLING MIGHT LEAK THROUGH, BRUSH THE BLIND-BAKED PASTRY WITH LIGHTLY BEATEN EGG WHITE BEFORE RETURNING IT TO THE OVEN FOR THE FINAL 5 MINUTES.

Fish Stock

Makes 1.5 litres

Good fish stock is notoriously difficult to buy unless you live next door to a good fishmonger. It's a great idea to get used to making your own.

250g mixed flat fish bones (brill, turbot, plaice), no heads

30g butter

1 onion, chopped

3 stalks celery, chopped

1 leek, chopped

1 bouquet garni (parsley, thyme, bay leaf)

10 whole black peppercorns

1.5 litres water (approximately)

1 Rinse the fish bones, removing any traces of blood.

2 Heat the butter in a large saucepan and gently sweat the onion, celery and leek until softened.

3 Add the bouquet garni, peppercorns and enough water to just cover the fish bones.

4 Cover and bring to the boil before cooking on a gentle simmer, uncovered, for 20 minutes. Skim off any cooking foam.

5 Turn off the heat and strain the liquid into a bowl. Cool the stock rapidly by placing the bowl in a bath of iced water.

6 Once cold, pour into ice cube trays and freeze for up to 3 weeks.

POUR THE COLD STOCK INTO ICE CUBE TRAYS OR ZIPLOC BAGS AND STORE IN THE FREEZER FOR UP TO 3 WEEKS. SIMPLY POP THE FROZEN STOCK CUBES INTO RISOTTOS, PAELLAS AND CHOWDERS.

Fruit Coulis

Coulis adds glamour when added decoratively to desserts. Invest in a squeezy bottle for restaurant-standard drizzles.

250g fresh (or thawed frozen)
  raspberries or mixed berries

55g caster sugar

50ml water

lemon juice, to taste

1 Liquidise the berries in a food processor.
2 Make the sugar syrup by dissolving the sugar in the water over a low heat. Once the sugar is fully dissolved, bring to the boil (without stirring) and simmer for 5 minutes, until syrupy.
3 Pour the syrup over the berries in the processor and liquidise to a smooth purée.
4 Pass through a fine sieve to remove any seeds. Adjust the taste with lemon juice or a pinch of sugar, if required.

OUR PREFERENCE IS TO USE MIXED BERRIES, AS USING ONLY STRAWBERRIES WILL PRODUCE A VERY PALLID AND SLIGHTLY LESS APPETISING SAUCE.

Dressings

Invest in a small whisk for making dressings.

Classic French Dressing

1 tbsp white wine vinegar

6 tbsp good-quality extra virgin olive oil

$^1\!/_2$ tsp Dijon mustard

1 tsp honey

sea salt and freshly cracked black pepper

1 Combine all the dressing ingredients. Season to taste.

Honey Mustard Dressing

3 tbsp good-quality extra virgin olive oil

2 tbsp lemon juice

1 tsp Dijon mustard

2 tsp honey

1 clove garlic, peeled

sea salt and freshly cracked black pepper

1 Whisk all the dressing ingredients (except the garlic) together, adjusting the sweetness to your taste by adding more honey, if required. Add the garlic clove.

Lemon Thyme Vinaigrette

1 clove garlic, crushed

1 shallot, minced

$^1\!/_2$ tsp Dijon mustard

$^1\!/_2$ tsp honey

1 tbsp red wine vinegar

6 tbsp extra virgin olive oil

2 sprigs lemon thyme, leaves only, or parsley, minced

salt and freshly cracked black pepper

1 Combine the dressing ingredients (except the herbs) and season with salt and pepper. Lastly, add the minced herbs.

Maple Syrup Dressing

1 clove garlic

1 tsp grainy mustard

1 tbsp maple syrup

2 tbsp white wine vinegar

8 tbsp extra virgin olive oil

sea salt and freshly cracked
black pepper

1 Whisk together the dressing ingredients and season with salt and pepper.

Rice Wine Dressing

60ml rice vinegar

25g caster sugar

$^1/_2$ red chilli, deseeded and finely
chopped

1 garlic clove, finely chopped

1 Heat the vinegar and sugar in a small non-reactive saucepan. Add the chilli and garlic and stir until the sugar is dissolved. Remove from the heat and allow to cool.

Coconut Milk Dressing

3 tbsp lime juice

2 tbsp coconut milk

$^1/_2$–1 tbsp fish sauce

1 tbsp sweet chilli sauce

sea salt and freshly cracked
black pepper

1 Combine all the dressing ingredients and whisk well.

Hollandaise Sauce

Serves 4

1 shallot, finely chopped

30ml white wine vinegar

25ml water

1 tsp peppercorns

2 large egg yolks, at room
temperature

225g unsalted butter, cubed,
at room temperature

2 tsp lemon juice

warm water, as required

salt and freshly cracked black
pepper

1 First make a reduction by combining the shallots, vinegar, water and peppercorns in a small saucepan. Reduce all the liquid to 1 tbsp, strain and reserve. Set up a bain marie and vigorously whisk together the reduction and egg yolks in a heatproof bowl set over the simmering water until a foam develops (ensure the bowl does not overheat by removing the bain marie from the heat when necessary). Whisk in 2–3 cubes of butter at a time, scraping around the sides of the pan as you whisk, until you have a thick sauce consistency.

2 Finally, whisk in the lemon juice, salt and pepper to taste. If the mixture is too thick, add a little warm water.

3 Once the sauce is made, it must be kept warm (not heated, or the sauce will curdle).

WORK WITH A BOWL OF ICE-COLD WATER BESIDE YOU IN CASE THE SAUCE GETS TOO HOT AND NEEDS TO BE COOLED DOWN RAPIDLY.

Tomato Sauce

Makes 1 litre

2 tbsp olive oil

1 onion, finely chopped

1 stick celery, diced

1 leek, sliced thinly

2 cloves garlic, crushed

2 x 400g tins chopped tomatoes

1 tsp sugar

50ml red wine

1 sprig oregano, leaves only

10g fresh basil leaves

salt and freshly cracked black
  pepper

Preheat the oven to 190°C/375°F/gas mark 5.

1 Heat the olive oil in a heavy-based saucepan and sweat the onion, celery and leek for 10 minutes, adding the garlic towards the end.

2 Increase the heat and add the tomatoes, sugar, red wine and oregano and simmer uncovered for 30–40 minutes, until reduced by half. Stir occasionally.

3 Season to taste and add the fresh basil leaves. Whiz to a smooth purée using a handheld blender.

FOR A SPICIER SAUCE, ADD SOME JALAPEÑO PEPPERS AND SERVE WITH LAMB KOFTA (SEE P. 109).

Mint Raita

Makes 250ml

220ml natural yoghurt

pinch salt

pinch cayenne pepper

½ cucumber, peeled, deseeded
and cut into small dice

1 tbsp chopped mint leaves
(reserve a tiny sprig for
garnishing)

1 In a bowl, whisk the yoghurt lightly until smooth. Stir in the salt and cayenne pepper to taste. Mix well. Gently fold in the cucumber and chopped mint.
2 Garnish with a sprig of mint.

....

TO DESEED A CUCUMBER, CUT IN HALF LENGTHWAYS
AND USE A TEASPOON TO SCRAPE DOWN THE CENTRE OF
THE CUCUMBER.

White Sauce

75g butter

75g flour

1.2 litres milk

salt and freshly cracked black
pepper

1 Melt the butter in a saucepan. Stir in the flour and cook for 1–2 minutes, stirring constantly.
2 Over a medium-high heat, gradually add the milk, stirring constantly.
3 When all the milk is incorporated, lower the heat, season well and simmer gently until the sauce thickens. Remove from the heat and allow to cool slightly.
4 Lightly press clingfilm onto the surface of the sauce and set aside until ready to use.

....

FOR A QUICKER METHOD, PUT THE BUTTER, FLOUR AND
MILK (COLD) IN A SAUCEPAN AND COOK OVER A MEDIUM
HEAT, WHISKING UNTIL THICKENED AND SMOOTH.
REMOVE FROM THE HEAT AND SEASON.

Perfect Rice

Serves 4

There are many different methods of cooking rice, but we think this absorption method is the easiest and once they try it, our students wholeheartedly agree.

340g (2 cups) basmati rice
800ml (4 cups) water
pinch salt

1 Rinse the rice in a sieve, rubbing your fingers through the grain until the water runs clear.
2 Put the rice and water in a heavy-based saucepan. Add a tiny pinch of salt. Cover with a lid and bring to the boil. Once boiling, reduce the heat and simmer (with the lid slightly ajar) until all the liquid is absorbed. You will know that the water has evaporated when small craters appear over the surface of the rice.
3 Cover and keep warm for up to 20 minutes before serving.

TO MAKE YELLOW RICE, SIMPLY ADD A PINCH OF TURMERIC TO THE WATER BEFORE IT'S BROUGHT TO THE BOIL.

Quinoa

Serves 4

Quinoa is gaining popularity in modern kitchens. This edible seed has a slightly crunchy texture and a light, nutty flavour. It can be substituted for almost any other grain, rice in particular.

300g (2 cups) quinoa
800ml (4 cups) water or stock
pinch salt

1 Rinse the quinoa in a sieve, rubbing your fingers through the grain until the water runs clear.
2 Place the washed quinoa in a saucepan and cover with the water or stock. Add a tiny pinch of salt. Bring to a boil, cover, then simmer over a medium heat for about 10 minutes, or until all the water is absorbed. Stir occasionally to prevent it from sticking on the bottom of the saucepan.
3 Drain of any excess liquid and serve.

QUINOA IS A COMPLETE PROTEIN AND HAS MANY HEALTH BENEFITS. IT WAS ONCE THE STAPLE FOOD OF THE ANCIENT INCAS IN PERU.

Basil Pesto

Makes 150ml

Nothing beats the evocative pleasure of freshly chopped herbs. Making pesto provides a truly heady sunshine sensation.

100g fresh basil, leaves only

25g fresh pine nuts

2 large garlic cloves, crushed

150ml extra virgin olive oil

pinch salt

25g Parmesan cheese, freshly grated

1 In a food processor, whiz half the basil leaves, all the pine nuts and garlic with half the olive oil (or grind in a mortar and pestle) until reduced. Continue adding the remaining leaves and oil and season with salt.

2 Remove to a bowl and fold in the Parmesan.

3 If the consistency is too thick, stir through more oil.

4 Pour into a sterilised jar and pour a thin layer of olive oil over the top. Seal the jar with a lid and store in the fridge for up to 2 weeks.

....

TO STERILISE JARS, PLACE THEM IN A SAUCEPAN AND BRING TO THE BOIL. BOIL FOR 10 MINUTES AND DRY THEM IN A HOT OVEN.

Index